JOURNAL FOR THE STUDY OF THE PSEUDEPIGRAPHA SUPPLEMENT SERIES

4

JSOT Press
Sheffield

Eschatology in the Theodicies of 2 Baruch and 4 Ezra

Tom W. Willett

Journal for the Study of the Pseudepigrapha
Supplement Series 4

Published by JSOT Press
JSOT Press is an imprint of
Sheffield Academic Press Ltd
The University of Sheffield
343 Fulwood Road
Sheffield S10 3BP
England

Typeset by Sheffield Academic Press
and
printed in Great Britain
by Billing & Sons Ltd
Worcester

British Library Cataloguing in Publication Data

Willett, Tom W.
Eschatology in the theodicies of 2 Baruch and 4 Ezra.
—(Journal for the study of the pseudepigrapha)
1. Bible O.T. the pseudepigrapha—Critical studies
I. Title II. Series
228′.9106

ISSN 0951-8215
ISBN 1-85075-160-9

CONTENTS

LIST OF TABLES

ABBREVIATIONS

APAT	E. Kautzsch, ed., *Die Apokryphen und Pseudepigraphen des Alten Testaments*
APOT	R.H. Charles, ed., *Apocrypha and Pseudepigrapha of the Old Testament*
BASOR	*Bulletin of the American Schools of Oriental Research*
BJRL	*Bulletin of the John Rylands Library*
CBQ	*Catholic Biblical Quarterly*
HTR	*Harvard Theological Review*
IDB	G.A. Buttrick, ed., *Interpreter's Dictionary of the Bible*
Int	*Interpretation*
JBL	*Journal of Biblical Literature*
JQR	*Jewish Quarterly Review*
JSJ	*Journal for the Study of Judaism*
JSOT	*Journal for the Study of the Old Testament*
JTS	*Journal of Theological Studies*
JTC	*Journal for Theology and the Church*
OTP	James H. Charlesworth, ed., *Old Testament Pseudepigrapha*
RB	*Revue Biblique*
Sem	*Semitica*
USQR	*Union Seminary Quarterly Review*
VT	*Vetus Testamentum*
ZAW	*Zeitschrift für die alttestamentliche Wissenschaft*
ZTK	*Zeitschrift für Theologie und Kirche*

PREFACE

This book, a revision of my doctoral dissertation at Southern Baptist Theological Seminary, represents the synthesis of a variety of interests. My undergraduate studies introduced me to philosophical thought and the problem of evil or theodicy. An interest in eschatological speculation and apocalyptic thought was nurtured throughout my graduate studies. The relative paucity of studies in early Jewish apocalyptic literature was the final impetus.

Special acknowledgment is due to Page H. Kelley and R. Alan Culpepper for the encouragement and challenge they have offered, not only during the writing of the dissertation, but throughout my entire program of graduate study. Thanks to James H. Charlesworth for consenting to read the dissertation and for making many helpful suggestions which have been incorporated in this final edition. The person who encouraged me the most was my wife, Karen. Without her this project could not have been completed.

Tom Willett

Chapter 1

JEWISH THEODICY

The problem of why evil and death persist in this world has occupied philosophers and theologians from ancient times to this day.[1] The prophet Jeremiah in the seventh century BCE lamented, 'Why does the way of the wicked prosper? Why do all who are treacherous thrive?'[2] David Hume borrowed what has become the almost classic formulation of the problem of evil in English from the Greek philosopher Epicurus. 'Is he [God] willing to prevent evil, but not able? then is he impotent. Is he able, but not willing? then is he malevolent. Is he both able and willing? whence then is evil?'[3] As Epicurus's thoughts on the problem of evil were influential on David Hume, so the efforts of early Jewish thinkers to understand this problem have been influential throughout subsequent history, especially on other Jewish thinkers. In order to understand how previous Jewish efforts at understanding this problem have influenced the authors of 4 Ezra and 2 Baruch, this chapter will give a brief survey of the answers given by early Jewish thinkers as reflected in the Old Testament and early Jewish writings.

A. *The Definition of Theodicy*

The term *theodicy* can be used to describe the efforts to explain the problem of evil and death by Jewish thinkers from Old Testament times. This use of *theodicy* is in a sense anachronistic since the term was coined by the philosopher Leibniz in 1710. In his work, *Theodicy*, Leibniz proposed many arguments to explain the presence of evil, the best known of which is his theory that this is 'the best of all possible worlds'.[4] With this argument Leibniz sought to encompass all evil in one overarching rational theory. Christian theology has traditionally followed Leibniz in his use of the term and restricted the use of the term *theodicy* to a rational theory encompassing all evil. Walther Eichrodt, for example, when discussing *theodicy* in the Old Testament, insisted that *theodicy* must be a rational theory attempting 'to balance the present state of the world, with its physical and moral evils, with the all-inclusive government of a just and beneficent God'.[5] To avoid the anachronistic use of *theodicy* when applied to Old Testament thought, care must be taken not to transfer back the latter intellectual baggage of the term which is foreign to Old Testament thoughts.

In order to help avoid this intellectual baggage, the definition of *theodicy* to be used in this study will be a broader definition borrowed from the field of sociology of religion. Peter Berger classified any attempt to explain evil and death in terms of religious legitimations, of whatever degree of sophistication or rationality, as a theodicy.[6] This broader definition permits all religious attempts to deal with evil and death in the Old Testament and early Jewish writings to be grouped together under one heading. These attempts varied from efforts to justify God in the face of an apparent wrong (see the reason given for Josiah's untimely death in 2 Kgs 23.26) to efforts to explain why man is evil (see Gen. 3; man's sin is central, not God's justice).[7] The subject of these theodicies varied from the specific (Why did this evil happen to me?) to the general (Why does there have to be evil?). Some theodicies sought to explain moral evil (the doctrine of sin) and some to explain natural evil (the curse of the ground in Gen. 3).

A theodicy can range from a rational explanation to the complete abandonment of finding a rational explanation. Peter Berger proposed a rational–irrational continuum as a convenient classification system and his continuum will be used here to bring some order to the broad range of answers given to the problem of evil in biblical and early Jewish times.[8] The exact degree of rationality or irrationality is often difficult to determine, so the order given here is only tentative. The following discussion does not attempt to be exhaustive, only to give representative examples of the major arguments.

B. *Old Testament Theodicy*

The many attempts at theodicy in the Old Testament varied widely in sophistication and intent. This variation does not, however, make any attempt less profound or even less influential, since theodicies on both ends of the rational–irrational continuum are used today.[9] In the Old Testament the theory of retribution occupied the far rational pole and explained evil by teaching that man gets what he deserves.[10] The wisdom literature most often used this doctrine, though it is pervasive throughout the Old Testament. Prov. 3.33-35 amply illustrates this doctrine:

> The Lord's curse is on the house of the wicked,
> but he blesses the abode of the righteous.
> Toward the scorners he is scornful,
> but to the humble he shows favor.
> The wise will inherit honor,
> but fools get disgrace.

On the irrational pole are those theodicies which never give a rational explanation, but neverthless reach some resolution, such as God's answer to Job. These theodicies provided meaning through a religious experience and often offered no explanation of evil nor promised future happiness. Other theodicies promised that retribution would happen in the future, or explained suffering as redemptive, probationary, or disciplinary. Even within these categories are variations of sophistication and intent.

Retribution

The doctrine of retribution played a central role in the attempts at theodicy in the Old Testament. Almost all the attempts either assumed the doctrine of retribution or reacted to it. The modern discussion about the doctrine of retribution in the Old Testament was touched off by an article by Klaus Koch, 'Gibt es ein Vergeltungsdogma im Alten Testament?'[11] In this article, a summary of his dissertation, Koch attempted to show how the Old Testament did not teach retribution. Yahweh does not cause good to follow good deeds nor bad to follow bad deeds. Instead, good following a good deed and bad following a bad deed results from natural consequences: the good or bad actions, themselves, cause the good or bad consequences. Yahweh's role in the process is limited to guaranteeing that the moral order, which he created, will continue. Koch examined many passages in support of his thesis; one which clearly supports his thesis was Ps. 7.15-17 (EVV, vv. 14-16):

Behold, the wicked man conceives evil,
and is pregnant with mischief,
and brings forth lies.
He makes a pit, digging it out,
and falls into the hole which he has made.
His mischief returns upon his own head,
and on his own pate violence descends.

The extent of the reaction to Koch's thesis illustrates the persuasiveness of his arguments.[12] He has perhaps erred in his argument in assuming that the Old Testament is a monolithic structure with only one point of view. Koch is undoubtedly correct in asserting that the consequence is inherent in the act in such passages as Ps. 7.15-17 (EVV, vv. 14-16). He overstated his case, however, when he pressed such passages as Prov. 3.33-35, quoted above, into the same mold. William McKane, in his commentary on Proverbs, based his classification of the sentence literature concerning recompense on the presence or absence of God-language.[13] With Koch, he would see those proverbs marked by the absence of God-language as expressive of wisdom thinking with no specifically religious content. In relation to these sentences, no theodicy can be assumed.[14] In the case of the sentences which have God-language present McKane's conclusion contradicts Koch.

> In the case of these sentences, I find it hard to resist the conclusion that the antithesis of *saddîq* and *rāšā'* is a dogmatic classification and that it is expressive of a premise of Yahwistic piety, namely, the doctrine of theodicy. By a doctrine of theodicy I mean the assertion that God enforces a moral order in relation to individuals by rewarding the righteous man and punishing the wicked one.[15]

McKane's isolation of two forms of the doctrine of recompense in the book of Proverbs, one of a religious nature and one of a secular nature, had a basis in the rest of the Old Testament.[16]

The theory of retribution can be found in many forms in the Old Testament and seems basic to Israelite thought.[17] The wisdom literature clearly stated the doctrine in many contrasting statements about the righteous and the wicked. The prophets assumed the doctrine of retribution in their teachings about sin. The doctrine formed the backdrop for the Deuteronomic and Chronicler's histories. In these histories a problem with the doctrine became evident, though it is reflected elsewhere. The problem is the conflict between individual and collective retribution. The complete breakdown of the theory of retribution and the breakdown of the traditional Israelite faith comes to the fore in the book of Ecclesiastes.

The righteous and the wicked. In the wisdom literature, a persistent strain sought to affirm that the righteous inherit good and the wicked evil. Contrary to Koch, some of these teachings contain an implied theodicy. They do not explicitly defend God in the face of evil, but positively teach that the world is a moral order maintained by Yahweh. McKane's classification of the sentence literature in Proverbs isolated those sentences which have this implicit theodicy. For the wise the doctrine of retribution explained the present state of the world and affirmed the moral order in the face of apparent injustices. Some examples of this type of proverb follow.[18]

> The Lord does not let the righteous go hungry,
> but he thwarts the craving of the wicked.
> (Prov. 10.3)

> The wage of the righteous leads to life,
> the gain of the wicked to sin.
> (Prov. 10.16)

> The fear of the Lord prolongs life,
> but the years of the wicked will be short.
> (Prov. 10.27)

It is plain that these passages reflect a religious attitude towards life and that the wise man who composed them expected Yahweh to vindicate the righteous rather than expecting vindication to come naturally.

The wisdom psalms also carried out this motif of the righteous and the wicked. Psalm 37 is an excellent example.[19]

> Yet a little while, and the wicked will be no more;
> though you look well at his place, he will not be there.
> But the meek shall possess the land,
> and delight themselves in abundant prosperity.
> (Ps. 37.10-11)

The author of the psalm zealously emphasized the traditional teaching to the point of absurdity in v. 25:

> I have been young, and now am old;
> yet I have not seen the righteous forsaken
> or his children begging bread.

The doctrine of retribution, when strictly held, turns the problem of evil on its head. Humanity, by its actions, determines its own destiny and thus the culpability of God is excluded. Its failure to experience good becomes humanity's problem.[20] For the wise the doctrine of retribution became the vehicle whereby a human being could shape his/her own destiny: if s/he wanted to experience good, s/he had only to act in such a manner to bring this about. For the prophets and others who had a more religious attitude, the doctrine of retribution was developed into the doctrine of sin. The aim of theodicy then became an effort to explain the evilness of humanity.

Sin. The prophets stress repeatedly that the reason for the misfortunes of the nation is the nation's sin.

> 'Yet your people say, "The way of the Lord is not just"; when it is their own way that is not just. When the righteous turns from his righteousness, and commits iniquity, he shall die for it. And when the wicked turns from his wickedness, and does what is lawful and right, he shall live by it. Yet you say, "The way of the Lord is not just". O house of Israel, I will judge each of you according to his ways' (Ezek. 33.17-20).

In this passage the prophet defends the justice of God by asserting that God acts according to the doctrine of retribution; the problem resides with the people. He stresses that the misfortunes of the people result from the injustice of the people and not the injustice of God. The prophetic use of the doctrine of retribution differs from the use in the wisdom literature examined earlier. The teaching of retribution, for the wise man, not only explained reality but could also be used to shape a person's fortunes. For the prophet, however, retribution served to explain reality in terms of God and his activity.[21]

The prophetic stress on human sin placed all guilt for evil squarely on human shoulders and in such a context theories about the origin of sin arose. Both Genesis 3 and 6.1-4 attempted to give an explanation of the origin of sin and as such their concern was with humanity. Genesis 3 both condemned and exonerated humanity. Man's guilt was assumed, but the guilt was shared with the serpent, the woman, and for later men, Adam.[22] Thus even though man was guilty, he was not solely responsible. Gen. 6.1-4 also dealt with the problem of man's evilness; here the guilt was shared with the 'sons of God'.

The prophets could also use the doctrine of sin to explain a specific instance of evil. The prophets Haggai and Zechariah, for example, attributed the misfortunes of those who returned from exile to their failure to rebuild the temple.[23] Hag. 1.7-11 illustrates this:

> 'Thus says the Lord of hosts: consider how you have fared. Go up to the hills and bring wood and build the house, that I may take pleasure in it and that I may appear in my glory, says the Lord. You have looked for much, and, lo, it came to little; and when you brought it home, I blew it away. Why? says the Lord of hosts. Because of my house that lies in ruins, while you busy yourselves each with his own house. Therefore the heavens above you have withheld the dew, and the earth has withheld its produce. And I have called for a drought upon the land and the hills, upon the grain, the new wine, the oil, upon what the ground brings forth, upon men and cattle, and upon all their labors'.

This conception of sin as the reason for misfortune[24] eventually led to the corollary that misfortune implied sin. This can be clearly seen in the discourses of the friends of Job. Job's friends, in their efforts to comfort him, ended up condemning him and trying to convince him that the reason for his problems was his own sin. Take, for example, a portion of the third discourse of Eliphaz.

> Is not your wickedness great?
> There is no end to your iniquities.
>
> Therefore snares are round about you,
> and sudden terror overwhelms you;
> your light is darkened, so that you cannot see,
> and a flood of waters covers you.
>
> Agree with God, and be at peace;
> thereby good will come to you.
>
> (Job 22.5, 10, 11, 21)

The idea that misfortunes implies guilt probably lies behind many of the protestations of innocence or complaints about taunters in the Psalms.[25]

> And when one comes to see me, he utters empty words,
> while his heart gathers mischief;
> when he goes out, he tells it abroad.
> All who hate me whisper together about me;
> they imagine the worst for me.
>
> (Ps. 41.6-7; Heb. vv. 7-8)

More in number than the hairs of my head
are those who hate me without cause;
mighty are those who would destroy me,
those who attack me with lies.
What I did not steal
must I now restore?

Insults have broken my heart,
so that I am in despair.
I looked for pity, but there was none;
and for comforters, but I found none.
They gave me poison for food,
and for my thirst they gave me vinegar to drink.
(Ps. 69.4, 20-21; Heb. vv. 5, 21-22)

Let them be appalled because of their shame
who say, 'Aha, Aha!'
(Ps. 70.3; Heb. v. 4)

These examples show how the doctrine of retribution could become the basis for a self-righteous condemnation of the sufferer. In these cases the doctrine not only exonerated God but condemned the sufferer.

The Deuteronomic and Chronicler's histories. In a narrative context, the doctrine of retribution assumed central importance in the Deuteronomic and Chronicler's histories.[26] In these sacred histories the misfortunes of the nation were always attributed to the sins of the nation and the king. The story of the tragic death of Josiah shows clearly how strictly the doctrine was held. The Deuteronomic historian testified concerning Josiah:

> Before him there was no king like him, who turned to the Lord with all his heart and with all his soul and with all his might, according to all the law of Moses; nor did any arise like him after him (2 Kgs 23.25).

In spite of the great righteousness of Josiah, he met an untimely death at the hand of Pharaoh Neco. The reason given by the historian, though strictly in accord with the doctrine of retribution, cheapened the story by its triteness.

> Still the Lord did not turn from the fierceness of his great wrath, by which his anger was kindled against Judah, because of all the provocations with which Manasseh had provoked him (2 Kgs 23.26).

The doctrine of retribution has not only made the story trite, but here has failed in its task of justifying God. Instead, it has caused God to be portrayed as petulant and unforgiving. S.B. Frost noted the embarrassment the death of Josiah must have caused, especially as evident in the silence of Jeremiah on the subject, and called it a 'conspiracy of silence'.[27] This silence points to the problem which the death of Josiah must have caused for the doctrine of retribution. This problem did not cause the Deuteronomic historian to abandon the doctrine.

A further development of this type of historiography can be seen in the Chronicler's history. The Chronicler proceeded to explain not only the untimely death of Josiah, but also recognized the contradiction in the long life of Manasseh. 2 Chron. 35.20-24 suggested that Josiah's death was a result of his sin in not listening to the word of God from the mouth of Pharaoh Neco.

> After all this, when Josiah had prepared the temple, Neco king of Egypt went up to fight at Carchemish on the Euphrates and Josiah went out against him. But he sent envoys to him, saying, 'What have we to do with each other, king of Judah? I am not coming against you this day, but against the house with which I am at war; and God has commanded me to make haste. Cease opposing God, who is with me, lest he destroy you'. Nevertheless Josiah would not turn away from him, but disguised himself in order to fight with him. He did not listen to the words of Neco from the mouth of God, but joined battle in the plain of Megiddo. And the archers shot King Josiah; and the king said to his servants, 'Take my away, for I am badly wounded'.... And he died, and was buried in the tombs of his fathers (2 Chron. 35.20-24).

Josiah was killed for this one sin after the great passover which he ordered prepared. 'No passover like it had been kept in Israel since the days of Samuel the prophet; none of the kings of Israel had kept such a passover....'[28]

The wicked king Manasseh, however, who 'seduced Judah and the inhabitants of Jerusalem, so that they did more evil than the nations whom the Lord destroyed before the people of Israel', lived a long life.[29] To explain this the Chronicler tells how after Manasseh was captured and taken to Babylon,

> when he was in distress he entreated the favor of the Lord his God and humbled himself greatly before the God of his fathers. He

> prayed to him, and God received his entreaty and heard his supplication and brought him again to Jerusalem into his kingdom. Then Manasseh knew that the Lord was God (2 Chron. 33.12-13).

These examples show how the theory of retribution was used to explain history, even when history did not conform to the theory. The blame for the misfortunes of the nation was always attributed to the sins of the nation or the king. The motive behind the systematizing of history under the doctrine of retribution appears to be the removing of all blame from God for the misfortunes of the nation. This effort failed, as seen above, concerning the death of Josiah.[30]

The collective and the individual. As just seen, many times evil was explained as a result of the sin of the nation. This meant that the whole nation suffered, even the righteous, for the sin of the nation as a whole. In the story of Josiah, the Deuteronomic historian identified Josiah with the nation to the point that the past sins of the nation resulted in the untimely death of Josiah.[31] In the Chronicler's history, however, the idea of individual retribution dominated, so that the long reign of Manasseh and the death of Josiah were explained in relation to their individual actions.[32] The tension between the ideas of collective and individual is evident in numerous other passages in the Old Testament.

Both ideas appear side by side in the book of Deuteronomy, with no apparent effort at reconciliation.[33]

> ... I the Lord your God am a jealous God, visiting the iniquity of the fathers upon the children to the third and fourth generation of those who hate me (Deut. 5.9).

> The fathers shall not be put to death for the children, nor shall the children be put to death for the fathers; every man shall be put to death for his own sin (Deut. 24.16).

More often, the two concepts of retribution came into conflict. Abraham's intercession for Sodom in Genesis 18 reflected this conflict. The classic text, however, is Ezekiel 18. Here the idea that the individual could suffer for the sins of the community, as expressed in the proverb, 'The fathers have eaten sour grapes, and the children's teeth are set on edge',[34] created problems about the justice of God.[35]

> Yet you say, 'The way of the Lord is not just'. Hear now, O house of Israel: Is my way not just? Is it not your ways that are not just? When a righteous man turns away from his righteousness and commits iniquity, he shall die for it; for the iniquity which he has committed he shall die (Ezek. 18.25).

Ezekiel's response to the problem was to assert the primacy of individual retribution and to reject collective retribution, thus accusing the people of misunderstanding the problem.

> The soul that sins shall die. The son shall not suffer for the iniquity of the father, nor the father suffer for the iniquity of the son; the righteousness of the righteous shall be upon himself, and the wickedness of the wicked shall be upon himself (Ezek. 18.20).

The conflict between the concepts of individual and collective retribution shows how the adequacy of the theory of retribution was questioned. This questioning led to different answers to the question, Why evil? Before we examine these answers, the complete breakdown of the theory of retribution in the book of Ecclesiastes deserves study.

Ecclesiastes. Qoheleth confronted the problems that arise when the theory of retribution is shattered by reality. He despaired of finding any meaning to life when the theory had broken down. Traditional wisdom taught that life generally moved with a certain order, formulated as the theory of retribution,[36] but allowed for occasional capricious acts by the diety.[37] Qoheleth could only see the capricious acts.[38]

> Again I saw that under the sun the race is not to the swift, nor the battle to the strong, nor bread to the wise, nor riches to the intelligent, nor favor to the men of skill; but time and chance happen to them all. For man does not know his time. Like fish which are taken in an evil net, and like birds which are caught in a snare, so the sons of men are snared at an evil time, when it suddenly falls upon them (Eccl. 9.11-12).

Qoheleth looked for order and testified that order must be present. 'For everything there is a season, and a time for every matter under heaven'.[39] However, he was unable to find that order.

> He has made everything beautiful in its time; also he has put eternity into man's mind, yet so that he cannot find out what God has done from the beginning to the end (Eccl. 3.11).

Qoheleth looked for justice and even though he could not find it, testified ironically that surely God would bring it about.

> Moreover I saw under the sun that in the place of justice, even there was wickedness, and in the place of righteousness, even there was wickedness. I said in my heart, God will judge the righteous and the wicked, for he has appointed a time for every matter, and for every work (Eccl. 3.16-17).

The end of the matter for Qoheleth, however, was that justice was not to be found in this life and there was no hope for a future life. 'So I saw that there is nothing better than that a man should enjoy his work, for that is his lot; who can bring him to see what will be after him?'[40]

Ecclesiastes cannot be called a theodicy, for when Qoheleth gave up hope of finding a rational meaning to life, he gave up all hope of finding meaning in any form. The pessimistic conclusion of Qoheleth, when he experienced the breakdown of the theory of retribution, was not shared by other Jewish thinkers who developed other ways to understand the problem of evil and to make sense out of their world. To these other answers we now turn.

Suffering as Discipline

In the effort to give a religious explanation to suffering, especially that perceived as more severe than the sin merited, Israel's religious thinkers often understood suffering as a disciplinary procedure.[41] This understanding of suffering often occurs in the same context as the understanding of suffering as punishment for sin. The two ideas seem to be related.

> But if you will not hearken to me, and will not do all these commandments, if you spurn my statutes, and if your soul abhors my ordinances, so that you will not do all my commandments, but break my covenant, I will do this to you: I will appoint over you sudden terror, consumption, and fever that waste the eyes and cause life to pine away. And you shall sow your seed in vain, for your enemies shall eat it; I will set my face against you, and you shall be smitten before your enemies; those who hate you shall rule over you, and you shall flee when none pursues you. And if in spite of this you will not hearken to me, then I will chastise you again sevenfold for your sins (Lev. 26.14-18).

This passage from Leviticus shows how the two conceptions of sin and disciplinary suffering stand side by side. In a similar manner, discipline as the reason for suffering also plays a part in the reasons given for the wilderness wandering, even though the major reason usually given is the sin of the people.[42]

This form of suffering can even be seen as a sign of God's presence and care.[43]

> My son, do not despise the Lord's discipline
> or be weary of his reproof,
> for the Lord reproves him whom he loves,
> as a father the son in whom he delights.
>
> (Prov. 3.11-12)

The idea of suffering as divine discipline has moved away from the strict rationality of the doctrine of retribution. Not only does it not presume to explain all evil under one rubric, but the problem of determining whether any particular instance of suffering should be put in this class belongs to the realm of revelation and shows the irrational element in this conception. Some attempt is made at explaining evil, however, and thus the rational element. The idea of suffering as divine discipline may not be a theodicy in the traditional sense of the term, but it functions in the same manner and is encompassed in the definition given earlier and thus will be considered an attempt at theodicy. It represents only the first of many attempts at theodicy which occupy the middle of the continuum.

Probationary Suffering[44]

An idea found clearly in the prologue of Job attributes some suffering to a testing of the sufferer's faith or integrity.[45] This idea can also be found in Deut. 8.2.[46]

> And you shall remember all the way which the Lord your God has led you these forty years in the wilderness, that he might humble you, testing you to know what was in your heart, whether you would keep his commandments, or not.

Describing the reason for the wilderness as a test of the people's faith contrasts with the normal explanation, the peoples unbelief or sin. Along with the idea of disciplinary suffering, it offers yet another alternative to the normal explanation. All three of these ideas, disciplinary suffering, probationary suffering, and suffering as punishment for sin appear related and often occur in conjunction with one another.[47]

As with disciplinary suffering, probationary suffering has both rational and irrational elements. It makes sense that God might test humanity. However, only with special revelation can any specific instance be explained this way. This type of theodicy provides meaning and not necessarily happiness or a good outcome, as indeed do most of the theodicies with an irrational element.[48]

Redemptive Suffering

The idea of redemptive suffering appears to have had a limited, though important, provenance. The suffering-servant in Deutero-Isaiah, the shepherd in Deutero-Zechariah, and Jeremiah's confessions all contain the concept.[49]

The vicarious suffering of the servant can be seen in Isa. 53.4-6:

> Surely he has borne our griefs
> and carried our sorrows;
> yet we esteemed him stricken,
> smitten by God, and afflicted.
> But he was wounded for our transgressions,
> he was bruised for our iniquities;
> upon him was the chastisement that made us whole,
> and with his stripes we are healed.
> All we like sheep have gone astray;
> we have turned every one to his own way;
> and the Lord has laid on him
> the iniquity of us all.

Whether these poems refer to a person or a group, they give powerful religious legitimation to the suffering encountered. The knowledge of the redemtive nature of suffering has the potential of giving great meaning to the sufferer's life. Whether suffering gave meaning to the life of the suffering-servant one can only guess.

For the prophet Jeremiah, however, suffering formed part of his prophetic office. He cried to the Lord, 'Know that for thy sake I bear reproach'.[50] Yet Jeremiah never received satisfaction from the knowledge that his suffering resulted from his office.

> Is evil a recompense for good?
> Yet they have dug a pit for my life.
> Remember how I stood before thee

> to speak good for them,
> to turn away thy wrath from them.
>
> (Jer. 18.20)

Instead he demanded that God bring recompense upon the heads of those who persecuted him.

> Therefore deliver up their children to famine;
> give them over to the power of the sword,
> let their wives become childless and widowed.
> May their men meet death by pestilence,
> their youths be slain by the sword in battle.
>
> (Jer. 18.21)

Jeremiah did not like what was happening to him, and was never satisfied with the reason for his misfortunes. In this sense the theodicy did not work; it did, however, acquit God of any maliciousness in Jeremiah's suffering. Jeremiah's suffering, unlike the suffering-servant, had no inherent saving or atoning power. The redemptive nature of the suffering came about through the redemptive nature of his office. Jeremiah's suffering is almost a suffering with God over the rejection of God's message instead of a suffering for or with the people.[51] As Jeremiah was caught up in the redemptive purpose of God, so was his suffering.

Redemptive suffering has moved far towards the irrational pole. The vicarious suffering form of redemptive suffering still has the idea of retribution in the background; the vicarious sufferer reaps the result of the other's sin. Knowing that any particular instance of suffering is vicarious, however, belongs to the realm of revelation and not reason. Suffering like Jeremiah's has moved farther still towards irrationality. The reason given for Jeremiah's suffering constituted an attempt to give an explanation for his suffering and thus to inject meaning into his life. Jeremiah, however, considered it an inadequate explanation which gave no satisfaction. Even though the attempt failed to satisfy Jeremiah, it did explain his suffering and should be classed with the other theodicies. As illustrated by Jeremiah, theodicies containing an irrational element become more subjective as they become more irrational.

Future Retribution

The idea of a future retribution, whether of a this-worldly or other-worldly variety, has been a popular way of dealing with present evil throughout Christian and Jewish history.[52] The tension, examined earlier, between retribution working on the individual or the community level has an effect on the form of this type of retribution.

Future retribution for the individual appears clearly in the wisdom psalms. Sometimes the psalmist, when faced with the reality that often the righteous do not experience good but the evil do, simply kept belief in retribution by projecting retribution into the future. These psalms admit that the righteous may indeed suffer but they assured the righteous that the hoped for retribution will indeed occur. No hint is given in these psalms that this is an other-worldly retribution.[53]

> Many are the afflictions of the righteous;
>   but the Lord delivers him out of them all.
> He keeps all his bones;
>   not one of them is broken.
> Evil shall slay the wicked;
>   and those who hate the righteous will be condemned.
> The Lord redeems the life of his servants;
>   none of those who take refuge in him will be condemned.
> (Ps. 34.19-22; Heb. vv. 20-23)[54]

Other psalms project retribution further into the future and hint at an other-worldly retribution. Psalm 49 seems to project future retribution beyond the grave.[55] Ps. 49.14-15 (EVV, vv. 13-14) tells how the end of the foolish is sheol, but the righteous psalmist declared his different hope:

> But God will ransom my soul from the power of Sheol,
>   for he will receive me.
> (Ps. 49.15; Heb. v. 16)

The rich man, though, cannot take his riches to the grave and thus gains no benefit from them.

> Be not afraid when one becomes rich,
>   when the glory of his house increases.
> For when he dies he will carry nothing away;
>   his glory will not go down after him.
> Though, while he lives, he counts himself happy,
>   and though a man gets praise when he does well for himself,

he will go to the generation of his fathers,
    who will never more see the light.
Man cannot abide in his pomp,
    he is like the beasts that perish.

(Ps. 49.16-20; Heb. vv. 17-21)[56]

Such a future retribution fails to bring about retribution in a real sense since it only promises that in the long run the fortunes of this world do not matter. After death, fortunes are determined by what was done in this life. No hint is given that the wicked might be punished or the righteous might be rewarded, only that the wicked's riches will do no good at death.

The prophets conceived of retribution most often in the collective sense. Habakkuk, for example, was not just concerned about his own personal fortunes but about justice in general.[57]

The Oracle of God which Habakkuk the prophet saw.
O Lord, how long shall I cry for help,
    and thou wilt not hear?
Or cry to thee 'Violence!'
    and thou wilt not save?
Why dost thou make me see wrongs
    and look upon trouble?
Destruction and violence are before me;
    strife and contention arise.
So the law is slacked
    and justice never goes forth.
For the wicked surround the righteous,
    so justice goes forth perverted.

(Hab. 1.1-4)

The answer Habakkuk received to his questions was that he must be patient and not lose faith: retribution will come. The verses preceding the famous 2.4b enjoin hope in the future, and the structure of the book fills out the picture.[58] Hab. 2.3-4 affirmed that the time had not yet come, but it would:

For still the vision awaits its time;
    it hastens to the end—it will not lie.
If it seems slow, wait for it;
    it will surely come, it will not delay,
Behold, he whose soul is not upright in him shall fail,
    but the righteous shall live by his faith.

The woes in ch. 2 affirmed that judgment will come and the final psalm, ch. 3, reaffirmed the necessity of faith, no matter what. Habakkuk's answer to his questions of theodicy was that retribution will happen and that he must believe that retribution will happen, no matter how it appears now.

Finding a clear reference to retribution in an other-worldly sense is difficult if not impossible in the prophets. In the Isaiah apocalypse (chs. 24–27), a frequently cited example of the other-worldly type of eschatology in the prophets, the context is clearly eschatological, but whether this eschaton will be in this world or the next is not clear.[59] Isa. 24.21-23 seems to have cosmic references and because of this could be referring to an other-worldly type of retribution (even the host of heaven will be punished):

> On that day the Lord will punish
> the host of heaven, in heaven,
> and the kings of the earth, on the earth.
> they will be gathered together
> as prisoners in a pit;
> they will be shut up in a prison,
> and after many days they will be punished.
> Then the moon will be confounded,
> and the sun ashamed;
> for the Lord of hosts will reign
> on Mount Zion and in Jerusalem
> and before his elders he will manifest his glory.

These cosmic references, however, could be nothing more than a use of mythical language to describe the coming victory of Yahweh. No matter how these verses are understood, they do point to a future event where the present world order will radically change, and if they do not speak of an other-worldly eschatological event, they lay the ground for such thought.[60] Other passages from the prophets also present such problems of interpretation.[61] That which can be safely said about the prophets concerning an other-worldly eschatology is the conclusion reached above for Isaiah: they at least prepare the ground for an other-worldly eschatology.

Theophany

The final type of theodicy found in the Old Testament can be described on one hand as the rejection of the ability of the doctrine of retribution to provide meaning, and on the other hand as the finding of meaning in an overwhelming religious experience.[62] The classic text in the Old Testament which struggles with the problem of theodicy, the book of Job, understood theodicy in this way.[63] In response to all of Job's pleading and questioning about his misfortune, he really received no answer; only the reader of the book in its present form knows why Job was suffering. The Lord's answer to Job is a theophany and a series of enigmatic questions which Job is unable to answer (chs. 38–39). When Job refuses even to try to answer these questions, the Lord's reply comes to the heart of the matter.

> Will you even put me in the wrong?
>   Will you condemn me that you may be justified?
>
> (Job 40.8)

The rest of ch. 40 and all of ch. 41 proceed to list some of the great activities of the Lord in the face of which Job can only stand speechless. This recitation does not convince Job of God's justice or answer any of Job's questions; it only overwhelms Job so that his problems pale in insignificance. Job did not find the meaning of his suffering, he found meaning in his overwhelming religious experience.[64] This type of answer to the problem of theodicy is no answer at all in the traditional sense, since it gives no logical explanation of suffering, but constitutes a profoundly religious answer to the problem.[65]

This type of theodicy can also be found in Psalm 73.[66] The problem addressed there resembles the problem of Job: How can belief in a just God be reconciled with the inequities of this life? The search for an answer to this problem had almost caused the psalmist to falter in his faith. The psalm starts with a traditional formula.

> Truly God is good to the upright,
>   to those who are pure in heart.
> But as for me, my feet had almost stumbled,
>   my steps had well nigh slipped.
> For I was envious of the arrogant,
>   when I saw the prosperity of the wicked.
>
> (Ps. 73.1-3)

It is not clear whether the psalmist intended the first verse as a true affirmation of his faith, as an ironic statement, or perhaps as both. The answer the psalmist reached constituted, at the least, a reformulation of this traditional thought. After a recitation of his problems, the psalmist concluded:

But when I thought how to understand this,
it seemed to me a wearisome task,
until I went into the sanctuary of God;
then I perceived their end.

(Ps. 73.16-17)

In the sanctuary, the psalmist came to realize that the end is without hope for those who do not know the Lord, but more importantly the psalmist found the presence of God, and in this find the answer.[67]

But as for me it is good to be near God;
I have made the Lord God my refuge,
that I may tell of all thy works.

(Ps. 73.28)

For both Job and the Psalmist the question of theodicy was answered by God's presence which overshadowed the problem of theodicy. In this type of theodicy, the questioner finds no answer but finds God in the process. This may be the real goal of the quest anyway.

C. *Early Jewish Theodicy*

Jewish thinkers from the early Jewish period continued to use many of the ideas of their predecessors to answer the question of theodicy. Sirach, the wise man, continued to teach the doctrine of retribution.[68]

Good things and bad, life and death,
poverty and wealth, come from the Lord.

(Sir. 11.14)

Whoever throws a stone straight up throws it on his own head;
and a treacherous blow opens up wounds.
He who digs a pit will fall into it,
and he who sets a snare will be caught in it.
If a man does evil, it will roll back upon him,
and he will not know where it came from.

(Sir. 27.25-27)

Sirach could also understand suffering as discipline from the Lord.[69]

> He who fears the Lord will accept his discipline,
> and those who rise early to seek him will find favor.
> (Sir. 32.14)

The author of 1 Maccabees taught the concept of testing. 'Was not Abraham found faithful when tested, and it was reckoned to him as righteousness?'[70] So the previous answers to the question of theodicy can be traced into the post-biblical writings. A few new answers did appear during this time which make a contribution to the resolution of the problem of theodicy. To these answers the study now turns.

Everything Is Good

Sirach, in his search for understanding about the world, came to the conclusion that if God created the world, then everything in it must be good.[71]

> The works of the Lord are all good,
> and he will supply every need in its hour.
> And no one can say, 'this is worse than that',
> for all things will prove good in their season.
> So now sing praise with all your heart and voice,
> and bless the name of the Lord.
> (Sir. 39.33-35)[72]

In terms of theodicy, this means that evil is not really evil, that everything will be shown as good in its time.[73] This type of theodicy can be called theodicy in the classical sense, and as such occupies the far rational pole of the rational-irrational continuum.

Future Retribution

The idea of an other-worldly future retribution became fully developed in the early Jewish period occurring in many different forms.[74] The wisdom of Solomon clearly teaches this doctrine.

> But the souls of the righteous are in the hand of God,
> and no torment will ever touch them.
> In the eyes of the foolish they seemed to have died,
> and their departure was thought to be an affliction,
> and their going from us to be their destruction;
> but they are at peace.
> For though in the sight of men they were punished,
> their hope is full of immortality.
> Having been disciplined a little, they will receive great good,

> because God tested them and found them worthy of himself;
> like gold in the furnace he tried them,
> and like a sacrificial burnt offering he accepted them.
> In the time of their visitation they will shine forth,
> and will run like sparks through the stubble.
>
> (Wis. 3.1-7)

Though death and suffering may seem unfair for the righteous, they receive their reward after death through immortality. The wisdom of Solomon carried retribution into the future life for the unrighteous also.

> If they die young, they will have no hope
> and no consolation in the day of decision.
> For the end of an unrighteous generation is grievous.
>
> (Wis. 3.18-19)

The idea of an other-worldly future retribution had come to full bloom. In the future life the righteous receive immortality and the unrighteous receive a grievous end. For theodicy, this doctrine means that in the future life all wrongs will be righted, and the justice of God and the righteousness and unrighteousness of man will be revealed.

D. *Types of Jewish Theodicy*

Theodicy has been defined here as any attempt to explain evil and death in religious terms. This contrasted with the traditional definition which considered only those theodicies which were strictly rational as theodicies, even though the same issues could be dealt with in ways not considered theodicy. The broader definition adopted here included these other attempts to deal with evil and death using religious terms and was used in the search for different types of Jewish theodicy. The theodicies found in the Old Testament and other early Jewish writings were classified on a rational–irrational continuum.

Two types of theodicy were classified on the rational pole of the continuum. In the Old Testament, the doctrine of retribution was found to be basic to old Testament thought and the basis for most explanations of evil and death. This doctrine taught that a person's actions, whether righteous or unrighteous, determined a person's lot in life. The book of Sirach proposed the idea that everything is good and has its purpose in God's creation. Both of these attempts to understand the world which contains evil and death are theodicy in the traditional sense.

The middle of the rational-irrational continuum contains a number of theodicies which are difficult to rank. The ranking given here is only tentative. The ideas of disciplinary and probationary suffering still have retribution in the background. They generally explain suffering which might be perceived as more severe than the sin merits. Redemptive suffering represents a further development of the idea of suffering. Retribution still stands in the background, but the sufferer now suffers for the sin of another. The final type of theodicy in the middle of the continuum is the concept of future retribution. This received its finished form in the early Jewish period when retribution was extended into a future life or existence.

The irrational pole of the continuum is occupied by a theodicy which abandoned any rational attempt whatsoever to understand evil and death. The sufferer found meaning in an overwhelming religious experience. Such is the answer Job found to his questions. Surprisingly, these are the basic types of theodicy still available to us today.

Chapter 2

APOCALYPTIC LITERATURE

The study of apocalyptic literature has been characterized by disagreement over the nature of apocalypticism and confusion about terminology. This study will therefore begin with a clarification of terminology. The following definitions will be used.[1]

Apocalyptic will be used to refer to the general phenomenon encompassing all three of the following specialized terms and the thought world reflected in the apocalypses.

Apocalypse will be used to refer to the literary works produced by apocalypticism.

Apocalypticism will be used to refer to the religious-social phenomenon which produced the apocalypses.

Apocalyptic eschatology will be used to refer to that particular type of eschatology which speaks of the consummation of history, as opposed to the prophetic concept of the coming new action of God within history.[2]

The attempt to answer the question, What is apocalyptic thought?, has taken two basic forms. 1. One form has concerned itself with the origins of apocalyptic thought. Its roots have been traced both to Jewish and foreign sources. Within Judaism itself, recent research has centred on the determination of the specific community in which apocalypticism arose and the examination of the general sociological matrix which gave rise to it. 2. The second approach concerns itself with discovering the essential form and content of apocalyptic literature. Here the discussion has centered around whether or not all apocalypses have a common literary form. Those who deny the common literary form usually characterize apocalypticism as a religious movement or complex of ideas.[3]

This chapter will quickly survey scholarly attempts to define apocalypticism. This will be done with two goals in mind: (a) to isolate those questions which arise in the study of the apocalypses for the evaluation of 4 Ezra and 2 Baruch in the final chapter, and (b) to see how the study of apocalyptic literature in general can inform the study of 4 Ezra and 2 Baruch.

A. *What is Apocalypticism?*

Before we turn to the specific questions about the origin and essence of apocalypticism, a brief survey of two attempts to answer the general question, What is apocalypticism? will be used to bring the issues into focus.[4] The work of D.S. Russell represents what could be called English orthodoxy concerning apocalypticism. The analysis of the state of scholarship by Klaus Koch presents the opinion of the German speaking world. Koch has sketched most of the issues involved in the current study of apocalypticism.

D.S. Russell

In the English speaking world, the ideas of R.H. Charles and H.H. Rowley have been very influential.[5] These ideas have found full expression in the work of D.S. Russell.[6] For Russell apocalypticism was a literary phenomenon born of social upheaval and persecution.[7]

> The apocalyptic literature is an example of the adage that 'man's extremity is God's opportunity'. It is essentially a literature of the oppressed who saw no hope for the nation simply in terms of politics or on the plane of human history.[8]

This social matrix left its imprint upon the apocalypses.

> The apocalyptic books constitute a record of these years, not in terms of historical event, but in terms of the response of faith which the nation was called upon to make. They cannot be understood apart from the religious, political and economic circumstances of the times, nor can the times themselves be understood apart from these books whose hopes and fears echo and re-echo the faith of God's chosen people.[9]

Russell found evidence of apocalyptic teachings in most Jewish parties and posited two major streams within Judaism cutting across all parties. One was the Rabbinic stream adhering to the law and the other was the apocalyptic stream building on the prophets.[10] Going against many earlier scholars Russell believed the apocalypses were written by a learned rather than poor or lower class of men.[11] Finally Russell described the literature with a list of major characteristics: esoteric in character, literary in form, symbolic in language, and pseudonymous in authorship.[12]

Klaus Koch

Klaus Koch gave a thorough assessment of scholarly research into apocalypticism including Russell's work and the work of influential scholars leading up to him.[13] The major value of Koch's work lies in his refutation of the biases against the apocalypses, especially in continental research, and in his form-critical analysis of the apocalypses.

Koch began his refutation of the biases against the value of the apocalypses by recalling the heritage of nineteenth-century historical critical scholarship. Under the influence of such literary critical scholars as Duhm and Wellhausen, a gulf was created between the religion of Israel and Judaism. For these scholars, prophetic religion as represented by the classical Hebrew prophets represented the true religion; the developments of legalistic Judaism, however, smothered the spirit of the earlier prophetic religion. The apocalyptic writers were considered imitators who adulterated the pure prophetism of the classical prophets. Under Wellhausen's influence, German Old Testament scholarship, in particular, has often seen little value in the apocalypses.[14]

British and American Old Testament scholars have taken almost the opposite path.[15] While accepting the distinction between the religion of Israel and Judaism and the connection between prophecy and apocalypticism, they did not agree that apocalypticism had adulterated prophetism. As a result they directed their research toward discovering and describing how apocalypticism arose out of prophecy. The heritage of R.H. Charles and H.H. Rowley was considered by Koch as dominant in the English world. Charles, like German scholars, contended that devotion to the law characterized Judaism, but he posited the presence of two streams within Judaism. One, with its emphasis mainly on the law, developed into Pharisaism. The other stream, finding its roots in the prophets, developed into apocalypticism.[16] Charles understood the strong ethical emphasis of the prophets as one of the chief characteristics of prophetism and considered apocalypticism as the preserver of this emphasis within Judaism.[17]

New Testament scholarship has also helped determine attitudes as to the value of the apocalypses. Continental New Testament scholarship, following Old Testament scholarship's attachment to the prophets, has considered Jesus the successor of the prophets. This estimate succeeded in elevating Jesus, for he was seen as the successor of the 'true' religion, and continued the denigration of apocalypticism which adulterated the 'true' religion. New Testament scholarship, however, has continually been confronted with scholars pointing to the relationship between apocalyptic and early Christian ideas. Thus the task of rescuing Jesus from apocalypticism has continually plagued New Testament scholars. Koch characterized the New Testament scholars' attitude toward apocalypticism as a series of waves for and against. Recent New Testament scholars have once again pointed out the apocalyptic roots of early Christianity and brought the problem to the forefront.[18]

Koch's survey of the scholarly attitudes toward apocalypticism brought to light many of the presuppositions of previous scholarship and served as the basis for his positive suggestions. First he suggested a group of apocalypses upon which to base studies. This group should include Daniel, 1 Enoch, 2 Baruch, 4 Ezra, the Apocalypse of Abraham, and the book of Revelation. Second, he suggested that before arriving at a binding definition of apocalypticism the prior work of form criticism and literary and linguistic history should be undertaken.[19] What he failed to mention, however, was his presupposition that apocalypticism is a literary phenomenon and that the apocalypses have a common form. On this point many would not agree with him, even though they would accept his first suggestion about the basic group of works to study. Christopher Rowland, for example, in his recent study would agree that at least those works listed by Koch should be included in the study of apocalypticism,[20] but after giving a brief survey of research he concludes:

> All this seems to indicate that we ought not to think of apocalyptic as being primarily a matter of either a particular literary type or distinctive subject-matter, though common literary elements and ideas may be ascertained. Rather, the common factor is the belief that God's will can be discerned by means of a mode of revelation which unfolds directly the hidden things of God.[21]

Paul Hanson also rejected the attempt to identify a literary type for all apocalypses. Hanson's study of the origins of apocalypticism followed the traditional English approach and investigated the prophetic origins of apocalypticism. In his study, the works he cited as examples of different aspects of apocalypticism included the works Koch listed as the ones on which to base a study of apocalypticism,[22] but Hanson also would not agree with Koch that apocalyptic literature has a common literary form. He listed three 'ill-fated' means of definition, the third of which was 'that which attempts to define it as a literary genre, since apocalyptic utilizes all the old traditional genres, transforming them into new, and often hybrid, forms'.[23] Paradoxically, Koch, Rowland, Hanson, and many other scholars basically agree on what works are apocalypses but cannot agree on what apocalypticism is, or how to identify an apocalypse.

In light of this paradox, Koch's initial analysis of the state of scholarship on apocalypticism may be correct. He suggested that the reason for the confusion lies in the failure to study the non-canonical apocalypses using the well established historical critical methods. Too many studies have not dealt with specific texts and have therefore misunderstood what apocalypticism is.[24]

B. *The Origins of Apocalypticism*

The search for the origins of apocalypticism has resulted in two basic types of answers. On one hand, the question of origins has been rephrased as the question of influences. The answers given to this question can be divided into Jewish influences and foreign influences. The major Jewish influences that been proposed are prophecy and wisdom. The major foreign influence has been identified as Persian-Babylonian dualism. On the other hand, the question of origins has resulted in the search for the sociological setting of apocalypticism, or Sitz im Leben. Almost every party in post-exilic Judaism has been proposed as the locus of apocalypticism. Some have given up on the search for the party and are content to describe the general sociological situation reflected in the apocalypses. The questions of influences and sociological setting are complimentary and both need to be answered to provide a complete picture of the origins of apocalypticism.

Influences

The influences upon the development of apocalypticism, both biblical and foreign, have been classified according to literary categories, because literature is the best reflector of the thought world of ancient civilizations. The Jewish influences have thus been classed according to biblical literary categories, and foreign influences have been listed according to categories used with foreign texts and ideas.

Biblical influences. Two major biblical influences have been proposed, the prophetic influence and the wisdom influence.

That apocalypticism developed out of prophecy has been the traditional notion of the origin of apocalypticism, at least for the English speaking world.[25] The differences betwen prophecy and apocalypticism have been noticed and analyzed, particularly the differing conceptions of history and the dualism of much apocalyptic thought, but the essential connection has still been maintained. H.H. Rowley has been a chief spokesman for this viewpoint and his often quoted conclusion has guided much research. 'That apocalyptic is the child of prophecy, yet diverse from prophecy, can hardly be disputed'.[26] The attempt to determine the exact nature of the connection between prophecy and apocalypticism, and the reasons for the differences between the two, have occasioned much research which has sought to document the connection between prophecy and apocalypticism.

With the effort to document the proposed connection between prophecy and apocalypticism has resulted in many parts of prophetic books being labeled apocalyptic or proto-apocalyptic, for example, the Isaiah Apocalypse (Isa. 24–27), Trito-Zechariah (Zech. 12–14), and often the whole book of Joel. Many studies have thus attempted to explain the prophetic-apocalyptic connection, but none has given the definitive answer.[27]

Much of the discussion about the difference between prophecy and apocalypticism has centered on their differing conceptions of history. Robert North has even called the differing perspectives on history the 'key' to understanding the difference between prophecy and apocalypticism.[28] Usually the prophets are understood as expecting God to intervene in history; they have a positive view of history. The apocalyptist, on the other hand, is understood as only expecting God to act beyond history, usually called a dualistic understanding, and thus has a negative view of history. The discussion surrounding this issue has been compounded by the confusion over the term *eschatology*, with some wanting to restrict the use of the term to references beyond history and others wanting to use it to refer to any reference to the future.[29] Much scholarly effort has been expended trying to show how the differing historical viewpoints of prophecy and apocalypticism came about, but the debate is far from over.[30]

The greatest opposition to the prophetic-apocalyptic connection has come from those scholars who understand the wisdom tradition as the determinative factor in the development of apocalypticism. Gerhard von Rad has emerged as the chief representative of this position.[31] He pointed out how the apocalyptic seers were continually identified as wise men or scribes; see for example, Dan. 2.48. Recognizing the differing views on history between the prophets and the apocalyptists, von Rad proposed that the apocalyptic view of history was closer to the wisdom view of history. For both wisdom and apocalypticism, history was observed from an outside viewpoint and seen as an example of God's ordering of the universe. Both also showed an interest in nature in much the same manner. As further evidence of the connection between wisdom and apocalypticism, von Rad listed the stylistic similarities and the common concern with theodicy. His views have been largely rejected, but they have forced many to redefine their views.[32] Even those who still hold to the prophetic-apocalyptic connection now admit some wisdom influence as well as others.[33]

Hans-Peter Müller has sought to expand upon von Rad's ideas by distinguishing between educational or proverbial wisdom and 'mantic' wisdom, which included such things as the interpretation of dreams, such as in the Joseph story.[34] By this distinction he sought to explain the eschatological orientation of apocalypticism, which is lacking in wisdom. Previous scholars had emphasized the 'mantic' or irrational origin of both prophecy and apocalypticism, thinking thereby to maintain the prophetic-apocalyptic connection.[35] The connection of prophecy and apocalypticism by the 'mantic' element has largely been superseded by the mantic-wisdom connection.[36]

Gerhard von Rad's insistence upon the wisdom-apocalyptic connection and the forcefulness of his arguments have caused scholars to take seriously the variety of different influences upon the development of apocalypticism. Hans Dieter Betz pointed out how the finding of the roots of apocalypticism solely in Old Testament prophecy constituted a major methodological flaw, since prophecy often became the only determining factor in interpretation.[37] The same criticism could be leveled against von Rad or any one else who tried to name the one major determining influence in the development of apocalypticism. The variety of influences proposed perhaps suggests that apocalypticism fed from a variety of sources with no one being determinative.

Foreign influences. In order to account for the many new features of apocalypticism, scholars, particularly on the continent, have often attributed them to foreign influences.[38] The older trend was toward a Persian-Babylonian dualistic influence, but Egyptian and Canaanite influences have also been supported.[39]

Martin Noth attributed the successive world empire schematization of history to Babylonian influences from the years 612 to 539 BCE.[40] Sigmund Mowinckel insisted upon the inseparability of eschatological thought and Iranian-Persian dualism.[41] More recent scholars have followed this thinking. William R. Murdock, after examining the conception of history in the apocalypses, followed Mowinckel in calling it eschatological-dualistic derived from Iranian-Babylonian syncretism.[42] The history of religions approach has maintained the Iranian-Babylonian influence. Hans D. Betz affirmed the Iranian-Babylonian influence on apocalypticism, but found all the things listed as typical of apocalypticism also typical of the whole period and present in all the surrounding cultures.[43] Apocalypticism should be thought of as the child of the entire age.

The evidence of foreign influence has been such that even those who have insisted upon a prophetic-apocalyptic connection have been forced to admit some foreign influence. Apparently in the minds of many, this also involves a value judgment: whatever is foreign is inferior. In an effort to pay just due to the foreign influences and still maintain the integrity of the prophetic-apocalyptic connection, two explanations have been proposed. The first admits the Babylonian-Persian influence, but considers it mediated by the prophets. Frost, for example, suggested that the prophet Ezekiel introduced the Babylonian ideas.[44] The second explanation contradicts the history of religions approach of Betz and others. Paul Hanson, following Cross's lead, attempted to discount the Babylonian-Iranian influence by an appeal to the resurgence of ancient Canaanite myths under the influence of Second Isaiah.[45] Once again, however, the all important prophetic-apocalyptic connection is maintained.

Conclusion. The evidence of many influences, both biblical and foreign, has led most writers to avoid dogmatically declaring any one source as the only or determining influence. H.D. Betz has wisely warned against the easy assumption that the presence of old material or fragments of tradition constitutes a continuity of thought, especially when the new material has a different structure and tone from the old.[46] The radical newness of apocalypticism as compared to previous Hebrew thought and the variety of possible influences which have been suggested, demand caution in the search for one determining influence. In light of this complex situation many scholars have attributed apocalypticism to its *Zeitgeist*, abandoning the attempt to find a more specific influence.[47]

Having surveyed the research about the influences on apocalypticism, we now turn to an examination of the sociological context of apocalypticism.

The Sociological Context

Alongside the attempt to find the literary influences which brought about apocalypticism has gone the attempt to identify the Jewish party or general sociological context in which apocalypticism arose. This endeavor first began with an attempt to designate the particular Jewish party out of which apocalypticism arose. The various identifications of the originating party have varied widely, however, with nearly every known Jewish party being proposed.[48] With so many proposals, many recent scholars have refrained from designating any originating party and have instead been content to describe the general sociological context which gave rise to apocalypticism.

Several important questions have emerged in determining a Jewish party or a sociological setting of apocalypticism. 1. What was the social position of the people among whom apocalypticism arose? 2. What was the attitude of the Jewish hierarchy toward this group? 3. Was apocalypticism confined to any one group or did it cut across party lines? To understand how these questions have come to be shaped and the issues involved, several representative positions will be examined.

The apocalyptic party. Nearly all of the known Jewish parties which existed during the period 200 BCE to 200 CE have been suggested as the locus of apocalypticism. All of these suggestions worked with the same basic data, but interpreted it differently. 1. The apocalypses seem to suggest a situation of persecution or crisis as their basic background. 2. Later Rabbinic writings reflect little if any influence or acceptance of apocalyptic ideas. This apparent rejection of apocalypticism by later Rabbinic Judaism led many in the early stages of research to assume that apocalypticism must have arisen within one of the many groups within Judaism who disappeared after the destruction of the Second Temple. Further research has shown that these basic facts give ambiguous clues to the identity of the party out of which apocalypticism arose.

One of the groups often identified as the one out of which apocalypticism arose is that of the Hasidim or Essenes. Otto Plöger advanced the thesis that the Hasidim, mentioned in 1 Maccabees 2 as those who joined the Maccabees to oppose Antiochus Epiphanes, were the party out of which apocalypticism arose.[49] F.M. Cross equated the Hasidim or the Essenes with those of the Qumran community, whom he also identified as the originators of apocalypticism.[50] Since the Hasidim were not of mainstream Judaism, an easy explanation for the later rejection of apocalypticism by mainstream Judaism was provided. A major argument against the connection between the Essenes-Hasidim and apocalypticism has been the presence of elements in the apocalypses which betray the concerns of a social class different from the Essenes-Hasidim.[51]

The presence of the wisdom influence mentioned earlier also calls into question the connection of apocalypticism to the Essenes-Hasidim, as well as any other suggestion implying a lower class.[52] A wisdom influence suggests an educated upper class in which wisdom thought could thrive. The somewhat esoteric nature of the apocalypses also suggests a setting in a learned class.

One Jewish party which could satisfy all the requirements mentioned so far is the Pharisees. The Pharisees valued learning and had connections to the lower classes. R.H. Charles proposed that the party out of which apocalypticism arose was the Pharisees. He divided Pharisaism into two branches, the apocalyptic and the legalistic, both having common ground in reverence for the Torah. The apocalyptic branch carried on the prophetic and ethical teachings and the other branch the legalistic.[53] Charles has rightly been criticized for this somewhat simplistic answer,[54] but he did point to some areas which have engendered continuing debate, such as the relationship to legalistic Judaism and the ethical content of the apocalypses.[55]

The apocalyptists' concern for the law, as pointed out by Charles, brings the issue of the relationship of the Rabbis and apocalypticism to the forefront, since the Pharisees are often considered the precursors of the Rabbis. The later Rabbinic writings reflect little contact with apocalyptic thought or with the apocalypses. From this lack of contact Louis Ginzberg wrote passionately and with insight trying to show that the Rabbis rejected apocalypticism.[56] Recent research has questioned the assumption that since the Rabbinic writings do not approvingly cite the apocalypses, the Rabbis were against apocalypticism.[57]

As with the search for the determining influence on the development of apocalypticism, the search for the group or party within Judaism in which apocalypticism developed has not led to any decisive evidence in favor of one party. Many recent scholars have therefore given up the search and have decided the evidence suggests that apocalypticism was current throughout all Jewish parties during its formative years. D.S. Russell spoke for many when he stated:

> We conclude that the apocalyptic writers were to be found not in any one party within Judaism but throughout many parties, known and unknown, and among men who owed allegiance to no party at all.[58]

Sociological setting. The inability to locate one specific party out of which apocalypticism arose, however, has not led to the abandonment of the search for the sociological roots of apocalypticism. Paul Hanson has worked out the most detailed suggestion for the sociological roots of apocalypticism. His analysis suggested that apocalypticism arose in:

> a setting in a crisis-ridden post-exilic community struggling to adjust to the loss of nationhood and tremulous under a new threat to the unity of the community in the form of a growing schism between two factions, one visionary and the other hierocratic.[59]

Even though his general analysis has met with approval and makes good sense of the literature, Hanson's two factions have not met with universal approval: he seems to have created two more parties after he has rejected the party approach.[60] Hanson's proposal reflects a common feature of many otherwise diverse attempts to identify the sociological setting of apocalypticism. Very often two diverse and conflicting streams within Judaism have been proposed.[61] Sometimes these streams have been identified with a party, as with Charles's two types of Pharisaism, and other times, as with Hanson, they cut across party lines.[62] Usually the conflict between these two parties is identified as the conflict reflected in the apocalypses. Michael Stone has warned against assuming that 'polemics or conflicts imply the existence of groups that carried them on'.[63] This erroneous assumption may account for much of the diversity in opinion about the party out of which apocalypticism arose and the sociological setting of apocalypticism. Nevertheless, the concept of a crisis situation which may have given rise to apocalypticism, whether or not this implies an internal conflict within Judaism, has found acceptance by most.[64]

C. *The Literary Form of the Apocalypses*

Are the apocalypses a strictly literary phenomenon or an accurate record of a religious experience? Very often the issue of the literary nature of apocalypticism finds itself in this either/or situation. For some the judgment between these two alternatives amounts to a value judgment. If apocalypticism is found to be a literary phenomenon then it is perceived as somehow less real and therefore inferior. The integrity of the visions recorded in the apocalypses then becomes the issue and is assumed that they cannot be real if they are found to be couched in a literary form.[65]

Attempts at Formal Analysis

The common literary elements and the shared subject matter among the apocalypses, plus the obvious differences from other literature, almost demand at attempt at finding the literary form of the apocalypses. These shared features account for the virtual agreement on what works are apocalyptic, while disagreement on the very nature of apocalypticism persists. The failure to define the literary form has contributed to the disagreement about the nature of apocalypticism, causing some scholars to despair at defining apocalypticism with literary categories and thus abandon describing it as a literary phenomenon at all.

The method of describing the apocalypses most often used and most often criticized is usually referred to as the listing method. Those using this method list the features which the works identified as apocalypses have in common. This method runs into numerous difficulties. 1. Too often the reasoning is circular: the list of common features identify the apocalypses and the apocalypses define the common features. 2. The list often is a mixture of common literary features and similar content. 3. No list has yet been offered which describes all apocalypses with no exceptions.

D.S. Russell has been an influential proponent of the listing method. He perceived some of the problems of the listing method and delimited his list to four major items: esoteric in character, literary (as opposed to oral) in form, symbolic (mythological) in language, and pseudonymous in authorship.[66] Russell's list is better than some but still inadequate for the definition of a literary form common to all apocalypses. On one hand, the listing method does not really describe a literary form, it only lists some common features. The composite nature of the apocalypses makes the delineation of the form difficult, but no more so than the composite nature of a novel or other literary work.[67] On the other hand, the lists do not apply equally to all apocalypses. This becomes evident when the individual apocalypses are analyzed according to a list.[68] According to some scholars the book of Revelation, for example, does not meet the criterion of pseudonymity.[69]

A major effort to define more adequately the literary form of the apocalypses was undertaken by a Society of Biblical Literature study committee. They concluded, subject to further study, that:

> 'Apocalypse' is a genre of revelatory literature with a narrative framework, in which a revelation is mediated by an otherworldly being to a human recipient, disclosing a transcendent reality which is both temporal, insofar as it envisages eschatological salvation, and spatial insofar as it invokes another, supernatural world.[70]

They further concluded that the apocalyptic phenomenon was not confined to the Judeo-Christian heritage, but found also Gnostic, Greek, Latin, and Persian apocalypses.[71]

The conclusions of the study group have had little more success in convincing people than the listing method examined earlier, and so the search continues. The present inability to describe the literary form of apocalyptic literature has led some to reject the essentially literary nature of the apocalypses. Others have simply abandoned the search for a common form.

Rejections of Formal Analysis

Those who deny the apocalypses have a common literary form can be divided into two groups. The first group deny the apocalypses have a common form, but admit that the apocalypses are primarily literary in nature. The other group would not only deny the common literary form, but would also deny that the apocalypses are primarily literary creations. This latter group makes the additional argument that the apocalypses are records of actual revelations, hoping thereby to establish the integrity of the apocalypses.

The first group, reacting to the current inability to define the common literary form of the apocalypses, recognize the literary features which call for formal analysis and therefore the literary quality of the apocalypses. Paul Hanson, for example, did not reject the idea of the apocalypses having a common form, but he did reject the present listing method as inadequate. The aim of his study was to clarify the historical and sociological roots of one feature of the apocalypses: apocalyptic eschatology.[72] He hoped, thereby, to cast light upon the confusion which surrounds the study of apocalypticism. Hanson has not rejected formal analysis itself, only the current attempts at such analysis.

The recent analysis of apocalypticism by Christopher Rowland can illustrate the other group which denies a common form in the apocalypses. He recognized the common elements among the apocalypses, but found the common ground not in a literary form, rather in

> the belief that God's will can be discerned by means of a mode of revelation which unfolds directly the hidden things of God. To speak of apocalyptic, therefore, is to concentrate on the theme of the direct communication of the heavenly mysteries in all their diversity.[73]

Rowland recognized both the common literary elements and the distinctive subject matter of the apocalypses, but sidestepped the issue of the common literary form of the apocalypses, by defining apocalypticism as a religious experience rather than a literary production. Rowland attempted, by his definition, to guard the integrity of the apocalypses as records of real visions and not mere literary creations.[74] This common belief, however, seems like a slim basis for establishing commonality and does not explain the common literary features.[75] The definition also falls heir to the circular reasoning of the listing method, since he used his definition to identify the apocalypses.[76]

D. *Conclusion*

The upsurge in research on apocalypticism offers hope that the mistakes of the past will be overcome and apocalypticism will be more fully understood. The evaluation of the place of 4 Ezra and 2 Baruch among the other apocalypses will be left to the last chapter. However, several points raised in this survey will be important for the following study of 4 Ezra and 2 Baruch.

1. The variety of different influences proposed and documented should give caution to any attempt to interpret the apocalypses by analogy with another tradition.
2. The question of the prophetic-apocalyptic connection has brought to the fore the differing views of history held by the prophets and the apocalyptists.
3. The possible connection to the wisdom tradition and their mutual concern for theodicy may give some hints to the interpretation of the theodicy arguments in 4 Ezra and 2 Baruch.
4. The inability to agree on the literary form of the apocalypses demands caution in drawing conclusions based on form alone.

Chapter 3

4 EZRA

Fourth Ezra is a Jewish work written soon after the fall of Jerusalem in 70 CE, but the literary context places the events in Babylon after the fall of Jerusalem in 587 BCE. Ezra the scribe is the main character. The book consists of a series of encounters between Ezra and God, or his angel, Uriel. These encounters define Ezra's struggle to understand Israel's tragedy in the fall of Jerusalem and subsequent captivity.

The attempt to explain the tragedy which befell Jerusalem and the Jewish people as recorded in 4 Ezra has been described as a theodicy. Fourth Ezra can be characterized as an attempt to involve the reader in the struggles of the character Ezra as he attempted to understand the problem of evil and thereby to present a narrative theodicy. This chapter will attempt, through an analysis of the structure of 4 Ezra, to understand the theodicy and the place of eschatology within the argument.

A. *Introduction*

To establish the proper background for the following study, a brief survey will be made of basic introductory matters concerning 4 Ezra. The conclusions reached in the following survey regarding the name, manuscripts and editions, original language, date and provenance, and unity of the book will be assumed in the study.

Name

The nomenclature for the various books in the Ezra tradition reached no consensus until modern times.[1] The work designated in this study, 4 Ezra, is chs. 3–14 of the work which most English editions of the Apocrypha call II Esdras. The name 4 Ezra was adopted to distinguish the apocalypse from the Christian additions contained in chs. 1–2 and 15–16. The modern scholarly practice of designating chs. 1–2, 5 Ezra, and chs. 15–16, 6 Ezra, has been adopted here.[2]

Manuscripts and Editions

The major texts of 4 Ezra were written in Latin and Syriac, with the Latin text considered the most important.[3] Other versions include Ethiopic, Armenian, two independent Arabic versions, plus fragments of Coptic, Georgian, and Greek translations. A modern edition of the Latin text, used as the textual basis for this chapter, was compiled by A.F.J. Klijn and published in the Texte und Untersuchungen series.[4] The Syriac text of 4 Ezra is available in the Old Testament in Syriac series.[5] The Ethiopic text, which followed the Latin text closely, was edited by August Dillmann based on ten manuscripts.[6] The Armenian and Arabic versions are rather free renditions and of less value for textual criticism. The Armenian version has recently been edited and published by Michael E. Stone.[7] The two major Arabic versions are commonly available in German translation in Violet's edition.[8]

Original Language

The attempt to recover the original language of 4 Ezra has received continued attention. Most students assume that 4 Ezra was originally composed in a Semitic language, the text of which is lost, and translated into Greek, the text of which is also lost. The evidence of the versions attests to the lost Greek version, since most of the variations between the versions and the internal evidence of the versions can be explained by supposing that a Greek text immediately underlay them.[9] Wellhausen, on the basis of Semitisms, argued that 4 Ezra was initially composed in a Semitic language,[10] arguing first for a Hebrew original, but later tending towards Aramaic.[11] Leon Gry gave the most detailed argument for an Aramaic original;[12] however, his conclusions have been largely rejected,[13] with recent scholars arguing for a Hebrew original.[14] Frank Zimmermann spoke for the majority when he outlined the genealogy of 4 Ezra as Hebrew–Aramaic–Greek–Latin.[15] A Semitic original has been assumed for this study, even though conjectural emendations based on this assumption have been avoided.

Date and Provenance

Most scholars would place the date of the composition of 4 Ezra somewhere around 100 CE. This understanding comes from the interpretation of the 'thirtieth year after the destruction of our city' in 3.1 and the interpretation of the eagle vision in chs. 11-12.[16] The 'thirtieth year' has been assumed to represent thirty years after the fall of Jerusalem in 70 CE, although the context purports to speak of the fall of Jerusalem in 586/587 BCE.[17] The eagle vision has produced a wealth of interpretations. Jacob Myers concluded that the eagle probably represented Rome, and the three heads were the three Flavian emperors, suggesting a date late in the first century.[18] Leon Vaganay, on the basis of the eagle vision, pushed the date down to the first of the third century.[19]

Two major suggestions for the place of composition have been championed: Rome and Palestine. The references to Babylon, especially in 3.1, have often been understood as cryptic references to Rome.[20] On the basis of the obvious Semitic influence and the author's concern for the plight of Jerusalem and the temple, a Palestinian origin has most often been adopted.[21]

Unity

The unity of 4 Ezra has been questioned since the turn of the century, when Kabisch, followed by Box, analyzed 4 Ezra into multiple sources.[22] They divided the work into five main sources joined together by a final redactor (R). The Salathiel Apocalypse (S) constituted most of chs. 3-10; chs. 11-14 included the Eagle-Vision (A) in chs. 11-12, fragmentary Ezra materials (E, E^2) scattered throughout, and the Son of Man Vision (M) in ch. 13. The source analysis, however, created as many problems as it attempted to solve and has been largely rejected. Most present-day scholars, building upon the suggestions of Gunkel, understand 4 Ezra as the work of one author who utilized various traditions fitting them more or less into a coherent scheme.[23] Gunkel suggested that the conflict within the work represented an internal struggle of the author: 'unser Verfasser aber ist keine abgeschlossene, zuversichtliche, wuchtige Persönlichkeit, kein Herr der Dinge, sondern eine zerrissene Natur, schwer beladen durch quälende Gedanken, im Kampf um die Weltanschauung'.[24] The tensions within the book represented the author's inner struggle as he tried to reconcile the state of the world with his faith in God, and are not evidence of poorly integrated sources.[25] A similar approach, first suggested by Egon Brandenburger, has been developed by Wolfgang Harnisch.[26] For Harnisch, Ezra represented a skeptical gnosticizing Jewish party against which the author polemicized through the angel.[27] Both of these approaches understood the different viewpoints expressed by Ezra and the angel/God as the product of the author and not the result of different sources. With Gunkel, we take the tensions within the book as representative of the author's inner struggle and therefore as reflecting his attempt to resolve his faith problems. The narration of the resolving of his problems is the theodicy which the author presented.

B. *Literary Structure*

The literary structure of 4 Ezra ties all the various parts together and gives them meaning within the whole. Since the work of Gustav Volkmar, nearly all scholars have agreed on the analysis of 4 Ezra into a seven-part structure.[28] Within this structure, section four marks a pivotal change in content and tone between the first three sections and the last three sections. The first three sections portray Ezra as seriously questioning God's justice and goodness, whereas the last three sections portray him as favored by God and receiving special revelations. Volkmar's analysis has been supported by Egon Brandenburger, who lists the following criteria for the division of 4 Ezra into seven sections.[29]

The opening framework

In visions 1-4 the following structure of the opening framework is found:[30]

1. The conclusion signalled by four elements
    a. A time indication (e.g. 5.20; 6.35)
    b. Response to the sorrowful situation: lamenting (e.g. 6.20; 6.35)
    c. Activity in preparation for revelation (e.g. 5.20; 6.35)[31]
    d. Response to an angelic directive (e.g. 5.20; 6.35; 9.26)

2. Introduction to the lament
   a. Dating formula (e.g. 5.21; 6.36; 9.27)
   b. The condition of Ezra's heart, soul and spirit described as distressed (3.2f.; 5.21f.; 6.36f.; 9.27f.)
   c. Formula introducing direct speech (3.3; 5.22; 6.36f.; 9.28)

The structure of the opening speech elements in visions 5–7 follows:

1. Concluding elements
   a. Time indication (10.60; 12.51; 13.58 and other places)
   c. Response to the situation (10.60; 12.51a; 12.51b; 13.57f.)
   d. Response to an angelic directive (10.60; 12.51a; etc.)
2. Introduction to the vision/epiphany
   a. Dating formula as before (11.1; 13.1; 14.1)
   c. Introductory formula to a vision/appearance (11.1; 13.1; 14.1)

The concluding speech elements

The structure of visions 1–3 follows:

1. Reference to the preceding revelation (5.20a; 6.30; etc.)
2. Announcement of further revelation
   a. Command with time indication, and special conditions: prayer/ lament and fasting (5.13b; 6.31; 9.25)
   b. Announcement of further revelations from the angel (5.13; 6.31; 9.25)

A comparison of the concluding speech elements in visions 4–6:

1. Reference to the preceding revelation:
   a. Retrospective: vision/meaning or both (10.52; 12.35; 13.53).
   b. Prerequisite: Ezra's worthiness (10.50; 12.36; 13.53b-56a).
   c. Meaning/result (10.55-57; 13.56; 12.37f.).
2. Announcement of further revelation:
   a. Command with time indication (10.58; 12.39; 13.56c).
   b. Notification of revelation of Most High (10.59; 12.39; 13.56c).

Brandenburger's list was very detailed, perhaps too much so if he intended to give the essential characteristics of the structure. The characteristics peculiar to each group of sections perhaps should not have been included in the list; for example, the different formulae introducing the laments (3.3; 5.22; 6.36ff.; 9.28) and visions (11.1; 13.1; 14.1). To Brandenburger's credit, he has noted transitional elements within literary units rather than just within the narrative connecting links, such as the retrospective reference to the preceding vision in 6.30 and the command to prepare for further revelation in 6.31. These transitional elements within the literary units show the literary unity of the book, and that it is not a compilation of various sources.

The application of these criteria to 4 Ezra yields the following outline.

I. 1st Section (3.1–5.20)
II. 2nd Section (5.21–6.34)
III. 3rd Section (6.35–9.25)
IV. 4th Section (9.26–10.59)
V. 5th Section (11.1–12.51)
VI. 6th Section (13.1-58)
VII. 7th Section (14.1-48)

This outline can be filled out by isolating the constituent parts of each section. The basic literary units which constitute the sections in 4 Ezra fall into three basic categories: narrative connecting links, speech units, and visions or revelatory experiences.

The narrative connecting links connect the basic literary units as well as the larger divisions outlined above.[32] The narrative links between the sections contain the majority of the criteria isolated by Brandenburger. For example, the narrative link between sections one and two (5.20-22) contains all of the criteria, except the command to pray and weep again in preparation for further revelation (5.13). The other major narrative links are: 3.1-3; 6.35-37; 9.26-28; 10.59b–11.1a; 12.50–13.1; 13.57–14.1a; 14.37-48.

A second group of basic literary units is speech units.[33] This group includes: prayers by Ezra—3.4-36; 5.23-30; 6.37-59; 9.28-37; 10.27b-28; 12.3b-9; and 13.13b-20;[34] dialogues/monologue between the angel (or God) and Ezra—4.1-47; 4.50–5.15; 5.31–6.16; 6.29-34; 7.1–9.25; 10.29-59a; 12.10-39; 13.21-56; 14.19-26;[35] and conversations between the people and Ezra—5.16-19; 12.40-49; 14.27-36.

The third group of basic literary units are visions or other revelatory experiences. This group includes: 4.48-49; 6.17-28; 9.38-10.27a; 11.1b-12.3a; 13.2-13a. The above analysis yields the following expanding outline:

I. 1st Section (3.1–5.20)
   A. Narrative introduction (3.1-3)
   B. Prayer giving initial statement of problem (3.4-36)

C. Dialogue with angel about issues raised by prayer (4.1-47)
D. Vision of furnace/smoke and cloud/rain (4.48-49)
E. Dialogue concerning interpretation of vision (4.50–5.15)
F. Conversation with the people (5.16-19)
G. Narrative conclusion (5.20)

II. 2nd Section (5.21–6.34)
A. Narrative introduction (5.21-22)
B. Prayer/complaint of Ezra (5.23-30)
C. Dialogue with the angel (5.31–6.16)
D. Oral revelation of the signs of end of age (6.17-28)
E. Dialogue concerning interpretation of revelation (6.29-34)

III. 3rd Section (6.35–9.25)
A. Narrative introduction (6.35-36)
B. Prayer/complaint of Ezra (6.37-59)
C. Dialogue with angel (7.1–9.25)

IV. 4th Section (9.26–10.59)
A. Narrative introduction (9.26-28)
B. Prayer/complaint of Ezra (9.29-37)
C. Vision of a grieving woman (9.38–10.27a)
D. Prayer requesting interpretation (10.27b-28)
E. Dialogue concerning interpretation (10.29-59a)
F. Narrative conclusion (10.59b)

V. 5th Section (11.1–12.51)
A. Narrative introduction (11.1a)
B. Eagle vision (11.1b–12.3a)
C. Prayer requesting interpretation (12.3b-9)
D. Monologue concerning interpretation (12.10-39)
E. Conversation with the people (12.40-49)
F. Narrative conclusion (12.50-51)

VI. 6th Section (13.1-58)
A. Narrative introduction (13.1)
B. Vision of man from the sea (13.2-13a)
C. Prayer requesting interpretation (13b-20)
D. Dialogue concerning interpretation (13.21-56)
E. Narrative conclusion (13.57-58)

VII. 7th Section (14.1-48)
A. Narrative introduction (14.1a)
B. Dialogue with God (14.1b-26)
C. Conversation with the people (14.27-36)
D. Narrative conclusion (14.37-48)

A preliminary analysis of the outline reveals several clues about the structure of 4 Ezra. Sections I and II share the common pattern of narrative introduction, prayer/complaint by Ezra, and dialogue addressing his complaints. These dialogues include a vision or revelation as part of the answer. Section III is generally similar to the first two sections but differs in some respects; it shares the common pattern of narrative introduction, prayer/complaint by Ezra, and dialogue concerning the complaint. The dialogue, however, goes beyond the questions raised in the opening prayer and lacks a vision or revelation like the first two sections. Section IV begins in the same manner as the preceding sections, except the prayer/complaint is followed by a vision and dialogue answering the complaint, much like sections V and VI. In each of the first four sections, Ezra initiated the contact with God, but in sections V and VI God initiated the contact with a vision. Sections V and VI have a similar structure, beginning with a narrative introduction followed by a vision; each has a prayer requesting the interpretation of the vision, followed by monologue/dialogue concerning the interpretation of the vision. The complaints are conspicuously absent from sections V and VI. Section VII is different again, beginning with dialogue and ending with a long narrative section. These observations suggest a 2-2-2-1 structure, with the first two sections closely tied together, sections III and IV transitional, joining sections I and II with sections V and VI, section VII being an epilogue. A more detailed look at the content of each section will confirm that the book has been intentionally structured according to the above plan and will show that the structure contributes to the meaning of the book.

Sections I and II

The first two sections set up the problem which the rest of the book attempts to resolve. The book opens with Ezra greatly distressed over the destruction of Zion and the corresponding prosperity of her enemies (3.1-3). The context places Ezra with the captivity in Babylon, on his bed, thirty years after the destruction of Jerusalem in 586/587 BCE.[36] As a result of Ezra's anguish, he pours out his heart to God in an anxious prayer about what he perceives as the injustice of the current situation (3.4-36). He recounts Israel's history, from the time of Adam to the descendants of Jacob, detailing how people failed in each instance to refrain from evil. This negative account of Israel's history serves as the basis for his complaint that people were unable to do right because of their evil heart:[37] 'Yet you did not take away from them their evil heart, so that your Law might bring forth fruit in them'.[38] Ezra compares the fortunes of Babylon and other nations with Israel's and complains about the inequity of the situation: 'Are the deeds of Babylon better than those of Zion?'[39] In response, God sends his angel, Uriel, to reply to Ezra's complaints (4.1–5.15). Uriel uses two basic approaches in attempting to satisfy Ezra. He first responds to Ezra's questioning with a series of rhetorical questions designed to impress upon Ezra the limited nature of his knowledge and to suggest that Ezra cannot comprehend God's ways and therefore should not question God (4.5-11). This answer does not satisfy Ezra in the least: 'It would be better for us not to be here than to come here and live in ungodliness, and to suffer and not understand why'.[40] Once again Uriel attempts to convince Ezra that human beings cannot understand the problems about which he is distressed because they involve the things of heaven (4.13-21). Ezra responds that, on the contrary, he is concerned about events on earth. Uriel, unable to satisfy Ezra with this approach, turns Ezra's attention to the future and the closeness of the approaching end (4.26–5.13).[41] The dialogue thus ends with a description of the signs of the end. Ezra drops his complaints at this point, though the next section makes it plain that he is not satisfied with the answers he has received. After Ezra's dialogue with the angel, he is confronted by one of the rulers of the people, Phaltiel, who accuses him of deserting or neglecting the people of the exile who have been entrusted to him (5.16-19). This presents an interesting parallel to the preceding prayer and dialogue. In the opening prayer, Ezra, in effect, accuses God of neglecting his people by allowing then to be enslaved to the evil heart and allowing the evil nations to prosper while Jerusalem was in ruins. As the angel brushes aside Ezra's complaints, so Ezra brushes aside Phaltiel's complaints. Section I thus presents Ezra's problem as the inequity of the present situation. He protests that God was unfair in punishing Israel, since the people had an evil heart which prevented them from doing good. When the angel tries to silence him by telling him that he is inquiring into matters which are beyond him, he protests that the things on earth are what he was interested in.

The second section reiterates the same themes as the first and has an almost identical structure. It, too, begins with an expression of Ezra's distress (5.21-22). In his opening prayer, he again complains about the inequities of God's treatment of Israel (5.23-30). Israel is supposed to be God's chosen, yet God has given Israel (the one) over to the nations (the many).

> And now, O Lord, why have you given over the one to the many, and dishonored the one root beyond the others, and scattered your only one among the many? And those who opposed your promises have trodden down on those who believed your covenants (4 Ezra 5.28-29).

The angel, as before in 4.1-12, answers Ezra's complaint initially by asking a series of rhetorical questions designed to silence him and communicate to him that he is unable to understand God's ways (5.33-40). These questions do not satisfy Ezra any more than the earlier ones. He questions the angel as to why God created successive generations instead of creating all people at once so the suffering would be over quicker (5.41-45). Using the analogy of women bearing children, the angel asserts the necessity of the succession of the generations (5.45-49).[42] Unlike the preceding section, Ezra changes the direction of the dialogue and asks about the end of the age: 'O Lord, I beseech you, if I have found favor in your sight, show your servant through whom you are going to visit your creations'.[43] He is told that God alone will visit creation at the end, just as he alone created the world (6.1-6). Ezra asks about and is told about the signs accompanying the end to the age (6.7-28). Even though the specific subject matter of the section is different, the basic complaint is the same as in the previous section. Ezra considers the present suffering of Israel unjust, especially in relation to the other nations. When he fails to get a satisfactory answer, he questions why the suffering encompassed so many generations, but once again the answer is the same: it just must be so.

Sections III and IV

The third section parallels the previous two sections, but with significant changes in structure and content. The section begins like the first two with a description of Ezra's continued grief (6.35-37). Ezra's opening prayer, this time, begins with an account of creation (6.38-54) as prelude to questioning God as to why Israel had not possessed the world made for her: 'If the world has indeed been created for us, why do we not possess our world as an inheritance?'[44] The angel again answers Ezra with a series of rhetorical questions

(7.3-17). The purpose of these questions, however, is different from the rhetorical questions in the previous sections; they do not attempt to convince Ezra that he cannot know the answers to his questions. These questions more directly answer Ezra's questions by telling him Israel must pass through tribulation to reach their inheritance: 'Unless the living pass through the difficult and vain experiences, they can never receive those things that have been reserved for them'.[45] The angel attempts to change the direction of the dialogue at this point toward the events of the end time (7.16), but Ezra will not turn from his subject. He provisionally accepts the argument as it applies to the righteous: 'The righteous therefore can endure difficult circumstances while hoping for easier ones'.[46] Matters are different, however, with the wicked. 'But those who have done wickedly have suffered the difficult circumstances and will not see the easier ones'.[47] The only answer Ezra receives to this question is that the wicked deserve what they get (7.19-25). The angel begins to tell Ezra about the Messianic kingdom and the end of the world (7.26-44). This description of the end does not turn Ezra from his questioning; he insists that all have sinned and the world to come will bring delight to only a few (7.47-48). With this addition to the argument Ezra changes the focus and broadens it to include not only the fate of the Jewish nation, but also that of humanity, for all have sinned.[48] In the background looms the question, not answered earlier (3.20-27), as to who could be considered righteous. Ezra continues, over all objections, to press his questions, but in the end receives the same answer: 'Many have been created, but few will be saved'.[49] Ezra, finally, can only pray for mercy for all, both righteous and wicked (8.4-36), as the angel reasserts the justness of God in bringing judgment upon the wicked (8.48-62). As in preceding sections, the section ends with a description of the end time. This time, however, Ezra objects to this proposed solution.

> Therefore, do not continue to be curious as to how the ungodly will be punished; but inquire how the righteous will be saved, those to whom the age belongs and for whose sake the age was made. I answered and said, 'I said before, and I say now, and will say it again: There are more who perish than those who will be saved, as a wave is greater than a drop of water' (4 Ezra 9.13-16).

Section IV begins much as the preceding three sections with a brief narrative introduction, and a description of Ezra's distress followed by a prayer in which Ezra raises his complaint to God (9.26-37). The narrative introduction signals a break, moving Ezra from his house, lying upon his bed, to the field called Ardat, where he breaks his fast for the first time. Ezra, in response to his prayer, receives a vision of a grieving woman (9.38–10.27a), instead of being engaged in dialogue—a pattern similar to the following sections. The vision portrayes a woman grieving over the loss of her son. Ezra attempts to console the woman and encourages her to rely on the justness of God: 'For if you acknowledge the decree of God to be just, you will receive your son back in due time, [and will be praised among women]'.[50] This action represents a break from Ezra's previous complaints and an apparent resolution of some of his problems. After completion of the vision the angel Uriel comes, in response to a request for interpretation, and explains that the woman represents the heavenly Zion and her son the earthly Zion; the death of the son is the destruction of Jerusalem (10.29-59a). This vision is a superb literary device showing the change in Ezra. He is now found comforting the woman over the loss of her son (Jerusalem), the very subject over which he has just exhibited unconsolable anguish. The section ends with explanation of the vision and promise for future revelations. Lacking from the fourth section, except in the opening prayer, are the earlier complaints of Ezra. The reason for the change, when it happened, and what this means for the interpretation of 4 Ezra are the central issues of understanding the book and are discussed in the conclusion of this treatment of the literary structure.

Sections V and VI

The format and content of sections V and VI differ radically from the previous sections, reflecting the tremendous change in Ezra. Indicative of this change is the contrast from Ezra's initiating previous sections to God's initiating these sections. Section V begins with a dream vision (11.1–12.3). Following the vision is a brief request for the interpretation (12.4-9). The interpretation of the vision, unlike the preceding sections' format in which dialogue predominates, is a divine monologue (12.10-39). This change from dialogue to monologue also reflects a changed perspective: gone are Ezra's complaints and questions, replaced with a seemingly unquestioning acceptance. The only hint of the purpose of the vision, within the scope of 4 Ezra, is given in Ezra's prayer requesting the interpretation: 'Strengthen me and show me, your servant, the interpretation and meaning of this terrifying vision, that you may fully comfort my soul'.[51] The interpretation of the vision comforts Ezra's soul and answers his problems. The section ends with another conversation with the people, who again accuse Ezra of abandoning them, much like 5.16-19. Ezra's response to them is unlike the earlier response in which he brushed their complaints aside; here he offers comfort.

> Take courage, O Israel; and do not be sorrowful, O house of Jacob; for the Most High has you in remembrance, and the Mighty One has not forgotten you in your struggle. As for me, I have neither forsaken you nor withdrawn from you; but I have come to this place to pray on account of the desolation of Zion and to seek mercy on account of the humiliation of our sanctuary (4 Ezra 12.46-48).

Section VI is much like the preceding section in structure and content. It, too, begins with a dream vision (13.2-13a), followed by a brief request by Ezra for the interpretation of the vision (13.13b-20). Unlike the preceding section, Ezra returns in this prayer to his previous manner of lamenting, but with a change reflecting his altered perspective. Here he laments what will happen in the future, not the present, and ends the lament with a positive comment: 'Yet it is better to come into these things, though incurring peril, than to pass from the world like a cloud, and not to see what shall happen in the last days'.[52] The interpretation this time is a dialogue, but this dialogue, too, is different from the dialogues in the first four sections and more like the preceding monologue (12.10-39). Ezra only responds to God once; this is no complaint but a simple request for further clarification (13.51). The dream vision and its interpretation function within 4 Ezra to offer assurance that God indeed controls the events of history as reflected in the final narrative portion of this section. 'Then I arose and walked in the field, giving great glory and praise to the Most High because of his wonders, which he did from time to time, and because he governs the times and whatever things come to pass in their seasons'.[53]

Section VII

The last section, unlike any of the preceding sections, has been considered an epilogue by nearly all theories of 4 Ezra's literary composition. Box suggests the present form of 4 Ezra was designed to commend it to the rabbinical circle of Shammai, with ch. 14 welding the name of Ezra to the book.[54] Gunkel considered ch. 14 an addition composed by the author designed to provide an aesthetically pleasing conclusion to the book.[55] Absent from this last section is any mention of Ezra's problems;[56] instead Ezra declares God to be justified in bringing destruction upon Zion (14.31-32), and the law efficacious in the saving of the people (14.34). No hint remains of Ezra's doubts and questions; he is full of praise for God.

Conclusion

Sections I and II share unity of structure and content, even though they do not exactly parallel one another, the structural similarities being the most vivid.[57] Both sections begin with a short narrative introduction describing Ezra's sorrow over the people in captivity (3.1-3; 5.21-22). Each introduction is followed by a prayer of complaint by Ezra (3.4-36; 5.23-30). Both prayers deal with the same general subject, what Ezra perceives as the inequities of the present situation of the Jewish people, and both use the same method to present their point, even though each approaches the argument from a different subject. In section I Ezra complains about the inability of anyone to do right, and sharpens the point by comparing the Jewish people to other nations. Section II shows Ezra accusing God of abandoning his chosen people in the hands of other nations. In each of the first two sections the complaint is followed by a series of rhetorical questions designed to silence Ezra by convincing him that he cannot understand God's ways and is foolish to ask (4.5-11; 5.33-40). In every instance Ezra is dissatisfied with the answer he receives to his complaint, and dialogue between Ezra and the angel Uriel about the issues raised by Ezra's complaint follows (4.1–5.13; 5.31–6.16). The internal structure of the dialogues is very similar in sections I and II: both are about the same length, include a visionary experience, and concern the present problems of the Jewish nation. In both sections also the dialogues end with a description of the signs which will signal the end times (5.1-13; 6.11-28). These descriptions of signs of the end function as an answer to Ezra's questions and close the dialogues. These two sections do not move the argument forward, but serve to introduce the problem with which the book struggles.

Sections III and IV are pivotal for the interpretation of 4 Ezra. It has long been recognized that section IV presents a changed attitude on the part of Ezra, but the exact point at which this change occurs has not been agreed upon. The analysis of sections III and IV just presented yield some instructive points. Section III has many affinities with the first two sections. It begins with a prayer of complaint answered by a series of rhetorical questions, tying it to the first two sections. The rhetorical questions function differently in section III, however, in that they respond to Ezra's questions. In the first two sections, neither Ezra nor Uriel will budge from their positions, but already Uriel has changed his tactics, in the succeeding dialogue, both change their positions. The dialogue in section III is very long and involved, with an important transition at 7.45 where Ezra changes the direction of the argument. Section IV also has some important structural elements giving guidance in its interpretation. Unlike the previous sections, Ezra does not fast in preparation for this encounter with God. In the opening prayer Ezra expresses his pessimistic outlook on life, but with significant elements of hope. The remainder of the section is structured more like the following sections with a vision and interpretation tying it to this last half of the book. Perhaps most significant is that in the last half, after the vision, the complaint and argument of Ezra are absent. Sections III and IV represent the pivotal area of 4 Ezra: structural elements tie them to the preceding sections and point to the later sections.

Sections V and VI belong together, having parallel structure. Both begin with a vision, followed by a prayer requesting interpretation of the vision and monologue/dialogue concerning the interpretation. The complaints of Ezra are absent and eschatological matters predominate.

Section VII can only be considered an epilogue. The last section is the opposite of the first section: Ezra's complaints are completely absent, replaced by affirmations of God's justice. The central topic is the restoration of the law to help guide people to the path to life, contrasting with Ezra's attitude toward the law in section I, where he considers it ineffectual because of people's evil hearts.

C. *Theodicy*

As the analysis of the structure of 4 Ezra has shown, Ezra's attitude shows a dramatic change after section IV. Following the suggestion of Gunkel, this change can be explained as indicative of the author's attempt to reconcile the present situation with his faith in God. This reconciliation can be called the author's theodicy. The previous analysis of the structure suggests a basic outline of the argument: sections I and II present a statement of the problem with which Ezra wrestles, sections III and IV show the resolution of this problem, sections V and VI illustrate the resolution, and section VII shows the result.

Sections I and II

The problem which Ezra confronts throughout the book is the subject of the first two sections.[58] The problem is given center stage at the beginning of the first section: 'I was troubled as I lay on my bed, and my thoughts welled up in my heart, because I saw the desolation of Zion and the wealth of those who lived in Babylon'.[59] These present evils cause Ezra great anxiety, and as a result, Ezra prays and recounts Israel's history from Adam to the Babylon captivity (3.4-27). The purpose of the account is to show the Israelites' continual inability to do right, attributed by Ezra to an evil heart. Ezra, through the evil heart argument, is protesting the standard argument that present distress is the result of sin. By stating that people are unable to refrain from sinning, the argument is turned back against God, implying that God erred when he punished the people, since they were incapable of doing right because of a basic human defect. Ezra further presses his point by noting how God endured and did not punish the sins of the Babylonians, while punishing Israel, who sinned comparatively less (3.28-36). Ezra, thereby, attacked the sin argument from another side, arguing that if God still holds the people responsible for their sins, in spite of their evil heart, then God is unjust because he did not punish the other nations in the same manner as he punished the Israelites. In response, the angel Uriel tells Ezra, through a series of rhetorical questions and a parable, that Ezra is incapable of understanding the ways of the Most High (4.1-21). This answer only accentuates the problem and is the basis for Ezra's further complaint that he is only trying to understand the things he experiences every day:

> Why Israel has been given over to the gentiles as a reproach; why the people whom you loved has been given to godless tribes, and

> the Law of our fathers has been made of no effect and the written covenants no longer exist; and why we pass from the world like locusts, and our life is like a mist, and we are not worthy to obtain mercy (4 Ezra 4.23-24).

Unable to satisfy Ezra, the angel turns the conversation toward the eschaton, suggesting by the change in direction that until evil is destroyed the righteous cannot receive their reward; only in the eschaton will retribution occur (4.27-32). The dialogue closes with a discussion about the certainty of the end (4.33-43) and the signs accompanying the end (4.44-5.13). Implicit with this appeal to the eschaton, though not explicitly stated, is the idea that Ezra's compliants about the present inequities will be redressed in the eschaton. The exact function or suitability of this description of the eschaton within the argument is not clear at this point, because Ezra does not react to this change of focus in the discussion except by dropping his earlier questioning. In the next section, however, Ezra again takes up his complaint showing that the talk of the eschaton has not completely satisfied his curiosity.

Ezra reiterates his complaints about divine inequity with his opening prayer in section II. He bases his complaint this time on the election of Israel as God's chosen nation (5.21-30). On the basis of Israel's chosen status, Ezra argues that Israel deserves special treatment; instead, he complains, Israel has received special mistreatment (5.28-30). This argument is a variation on the previous argument: God was unjust in punishing Israel, while not punishing other nations in the same manner. Once again Ezra is told through a series of rhetorical questions that he cannot understand what he is asking: 'He said to me, "Just as you cannot do one of the things that were mentioned, so you cannot discover my judgment, or the goal of the love that I have promised my people"'.[60] As in the first section a description of the end times follows Ezra's complaint. The function of this description appears to be much like the one in the preceding section; however, this time it relates to Ezra's complaint, telling him that present inequities will be straightened out in the eschaton: 'For evil shall be blotted out, and deceit shall be quenched; faithfulness shall flourish, and corruption shall be overcome, and the truth, which has been so long without fruit, shall be revealed'.[61] It even states that the evil heart about which Ezra complained in the first section will be changed: 'The heart of the earth's inhabitants shall be changed and converted to a different spirit'.[62] So the eschaton is presented as the time when the righteous and wicked will receive their rewards, and the major cause of present distress, the evil heart, will be changed. Once again, however, Ezra does not react to the discussion about the end times and the solution it presents.

The first two sections present the basic issues occupying the remainder of the book. Ezra propounds two basic argument, both aimed at the traditional argument that present evil is the result of sin. He first argues that God was unjust to punish people for sin, since they are unable to do right because of their evil heart. He then argues that God was unjust to punish Israel: first, because Israel's sins were no worse than the other nations', and second, because of Israel's chosen status.

Sections III and IV

Section III begins as the previous two sections with a prayer/ complaint by Ezra. Ezra this time uses the vehicle of creation to present his complaint, ending with the questions: 'If the world has indeed been created for us, why do we not possess our world as an inheritance? How long will this be so?'[63] Through these questions, Ezra has again accused God of unfairly dealing with Israel. This complaint is similar to the complaint in section II about Israel's chosen status. The angel offers his reply to Ezra's complaints through an allegory, suggesting that the present evils are the result of sin, and the righteous must endure the present evil to inherit the blessings. The angel's reply contains the two major theodicy concepts encountered throughout the book: (1) present evil is the result of sin; and (2) present inequities will be redressed in the future. Ezra, to this point, had never directly challenged the concept of future retribution, but here he objects to the justness of such a solution. With this objection the argument changes direction.[64] Ezra provisionally accepts the angels' answer as it related to the righteous, but brings up the more difficult circumstances of the wicked. 'The righteous therefore can endure difficult circumstances while hoping for easier ones; but those who have done wickedly have suffered the difficult circumstances and will not see the easier ones'.[65] Ezra, by not objecting, accepts the argument of future retribution for the righteous, but goes beyond normal questions of theodicy and questions the justness of future retribution for the wicked. This opens up the argument so Ezra can later lament that all people have sinned and are deserving of the fate of the wicked: 'For who among the living is there that has not sinned, or who among men that has not transgressed your covenant?'[66] In this way Ezra brings to the forefront the central problem of this section: in light of the universality of sin, what good are the promises of the future worlds?[67]

> And now I see that the world to come will bring delight to few, but torments to many. For an evil heart has grown up in us, which has alienated us from God, and has brought us into corruption and the ways of death, and has shown us the paths of perdition and removed us far from life—and that not just a few of us but almost all who have been created! (4 Ezra 7.47-48)

It did little good to say that the evil heart would be transformed at the end, as in section II, when the evil heart was the source of the present problem, and the deeds arising from the evil heart determined human destiny. The angel replies with his previous arguments: because of the evil human heart the Most High has made not one world but two, and the few who will inherit the second world are precious, and the many deserve the torment they will receive. This is no answer at all.[68] The argument has seemingly turned from concern over the present evils to the future destiny of man, but the reason for the change is that the future world is offered as the solution to the present situation. To accept the future hope as the answer to the present situation, the problem of sin, as it relates to the future situation, must be overcome.

Ezra's plea for mercy and the response he receives in the last half of this section are essential to his theodicy, for it is here that he most clearly addresses the problem of sin and the future hope. Throughout the book, Ezra's concern has been the nation Israel. His continued pleading on behalf of the wicked, after the admonition of the angel not to consider himself among the wicked, makes this clear. The wicked he pleads for are plainly the Israelites.

> 'About mankind you know best; but I will speak about your people, for whom I am grieved, and about your inheritance, for whom I lament, and about Israel, for whom I am sad, and about the seed of Jacob, for whom I am troubled' (4 Ezra 8.15-16).

Ezra begins his plea for national, not personal, salvation by asking

God to look upon the deeds of the righteous Israelites and ignore those who have acted wickedly (8.26-31). Ezra's plea for mercy recognizes that God's people have sinned: 'For in truth there is no one among those who have been born who has not acted wickedly, and among those who have existed there is no one who has not transgressed'.[69] Observance of the law thus is not the basis for inheriting the future glory.[70] In the same way, God will be declared righteous not when he equitably executes his law, but when he shows mercy: 'For in this, O Lord, your righteousness and goodness will be declared, when you are merciful to those who have no store of good works'.[71] In reply, Ezra is told that God will do as Ezra has asked concerning the righteous (8.37-40), but concerning the wicked he is told: 'Yet not all that have been sown will come up in due season, and not all that were planted will take root'.[72] This apparently means that God will save the righteous Israelites, but some of the wicked will be lost. Ezra's response confirms this understanding since he is not satisfied with the answer and pleads again for God to have mercy on his people: 'But spare your people and have mercy on your inheritance'.[73] In reply, God tells Ezra never again to compare himself to the unrighteous: 'Never do so!' (8.47). This is the second time Ezra has been told not to consider himself with the wicked (also in 7.76).

These admonitions serve a distinct literary function within the book. Only a superficial reading would suggest that they simply serve to further the Ezra legend by affirming the righteous character of Ezra. In both instances, the commendations follow a section where Ezra has lamented the fate of the wicked and counts himself among them. In the last instance, Ezra has declared all humanity guilty, pleaded for mercy, and declared that God will be righteous if he bestows mercy on his people, among whom Ezra includes himself. God's reason for considering Ezra praiseworthy is also instructive: not because he has obeyed the law, but because he is humble.

> But even in this respect you will be praiseworthy before the Most High, because you humble yourself, as is becoming for you, and have not deemed yourself to be among the righteous in order to receive the greatest glory (4 Ezra 8.48-49).

The net effect demonstrated in a concrete instance that God is merciful and therefore righteous. Ezra, however, fulfilling the role of intercessor for his people, continues to plead for mercy: 'I said before, and I say now, and will say it again: There are more who perish than those who will be saved, as a wave is greater than a drop of water'.[74] The angel's reply to this last plea affirms the justice of God upon the wicked and the great difficulty of saving any. Thus the section ends with Ezra's plea for mercy.

The fourth section gives a picture of the change in Ezra's attitude brought about by the previous interchange between the angel and him.[75] Ezra's opening prayer in the fourth section again concerns the fate of Israel as a nation: 'For we who have received the Law and sinned will perish, as well as our heart which received it'.[76] Again the fate of Israel, in light of her sin, is central. Ezra's attitude toward God, as represented by Ezra's attitude toward the law, has changed. Ezra can now affirm the glory of God's law, in spite of the judgment brought upon Israel by the law: 'The Law, however, does not perish but remains in its glory'.[77] Ezra's behavior in the vision immediately following this prayer illustrates the change in him. He attempts to console the grieving woman and admonishes her to put away her sorrow. 'Therefore shake off your great sadness and lay aside your many sorrows, so that the Mighty One may be merciful to you again, and the Most High may give you rest, a relief from your troubles'.[78] Ezra has moved from seeking consolation to giving consolation, and this final admonition to the woman mirrors the change in him. Significant in this admonition is the mention of mercy, which plays such an important role in the preceding section.

Sections III and IV represent the heart of the theodicy in 4 Ezra. Sin is suggested as the reason for present evil, and future hope is presented as the solution to present inequities. Ezra, however, has difficulties reconciling the two answers. If sin is the reason for the present miseries and universal in scope, then who can inherit the future hope? If no one has a chance of inheriting the future hope, then the human situation is hopeless. Ezra, however, finds a partial answer in the mercy of God, and God is justified because of his mercy.

Sections V and VI

Sections V and VI illustrate, through the use of visions and their interpretations, the future hope which Ezra has accepted. Section V contains a vision of an eagle and a lion, representative of the last world ruler and the Messiah. The vision describes the rise and the demise of the last ruler under the Messiah, and the deliverance 'in mercy' of the remnant of God's people. Ezra's response to this vision in his words to the people shows the purpose of the vision within the book. In contrast to Ezra's first encounter with the people, when he offers no comfort at all to them (5.16-19), in this section he offers comfort by assuring them that neither he nor the Most High has abandoned them. The declaration that God has not abandoned them contrasts with his opening complaints that God has abandoned Israel in the hands of the enemies.

Section VI offers another vision of the end times, this time in the form of a man rising out of the sea. The man has been sent by God to deliver the chosen people and gather them back together again. Once again Ezra's response to the vision gives the clue to its purpose. In sections II and III he complains that God has not delivered on his promises to Israel, implying either God's unjustness or his inability, but now because of the vision, he can declare that God 'governs the times and whatever things come to pass in their seasons'.[79]

Sections V and VI present a changed Ezra; his complaints are replaced by the confident assurances that God remembers his people.

Section VII

Section VII brings Ezra full circle. In this section he admonishes the people by telling them that their present sufferings are the result of sin, but future glories await them if they will rule over their hearts and minds. He describes God as the 'righteous judge' (14.32), in contrast to the earlier complaints in which he accused God of inequity in his treatment of Israel. To help them after he leaves, Ezra prays them for and restores the law to them through special revelation.

D. *Eschatology*

Two previous studies have dealt extensively with the eschatology of 4 Ezra, but the conclusions they reach are not compatible. Leon Vaganay, at the turn of the century, analyzed the eschatology of 4 Ezra, giving particular attention to the structure.[80] He noted two major transition points within the book: 7.15-16 and 9.13. He considered 7.15-16 the major pivot, with national salvation dominant in 3.1–7.14, and personal salvation dominant in 7.17–9.25. Vaganay, following the lead of Gunkel, suggested that the tension between these two poles was indicative of the author's internal struggle and concluded that the author was certain of national salvation but uncertain of personal salvation.[81] Shortly after Vaganay's study, Joseph Keulers studied the eschatology of 4 Ezra.[82] He suggested that sections I to III exhibit a concern for universal, other-worldly eschatology, whereas sections IV through VII have a national, this-worldly type of eschatology. Keulers sought resolution of the problems in 4 Ezra by separating the two types of eschatology.[83] With the suggestions of Vaganay and Keulers for background, a brief sketch of the eschatological teaching of 4 Ezra can be attempted.

Sections I and II

Section I presents a two-age eschatology; in the future age the righteous will get what they deserve (4 Ezra 4.27). The present time is a time of evil which will increase until the end, so the time immediately preceding the end will be a time of tribulation when righteousness will be absent (4 Ezra 5.2-13). The nation is clearly the concern in this section, and thus the eschatological material can only be considered national.[84]

Section II continues the two-age eschatology; the age to come is portrayed as the time when the wicked will be punished for their sins and the humiliation of Zion will be complete (6.18), a time when evil will be vanquished and righteousness reign supreme.

Sections III and IV

Section III offers the most complete eschatological picture of any of the sections. It introduces the Messiah, the Messianic reign, and the resurrection into the eschatological picture. At the end of the age the heavenly Jerusalem, the city now not seen, and paradise, the land now hidden, will appear along with the Messiah and his hosts (7.26). The Messiah will reign 400 years, after which he and all humanity shall die, and the earth will be returned to primeval silence. After seven days, the dead will be resurrected and God will sit upon the judgment seat (7.28-44). The state of the dead before the judgment is described as a period of torment for the wicked and a period of bliss for the righteous (7.75-101). The end is again described as a time when the righteous will receive their reward and the wicked will be tormented (9.1-13). Section IV introduces the heavenly Jerusalem, but its mention is not concerned with eschatological thought.

Sections V and VI

Section V presents, through the vehicle of the eagle vision, a picture of the rise of the last evil political kingdom, and the coming of the Messiah who will overthrow the evil kingdom and usher in a period of peace lasting until the final judgment.[85]

> For first he will set them living before his judgment seat, and when he has reproved them, then he will destroy them. But he will deliver in mercy the remnant of my people, those who have been saved throughout my borders, and he will make them joyful until the end comes, the day of judgment, of which I spoke to you at the beginning (4 Ezra 12.33-34).

Section VI speaks almost exclusively of the Messiah and his reign, this time through a vision of a man rising out of the sea. Before his coming will be a time of tribulation; accompanying his coming will be the revealing of the heavenly Jerusalem. When he comes he will judge the nations and bring the ten lost tribes together again in the promised land. He will destroy the nations and defend his people.

Previous to sections V and VI, the Messiah was mentioned only briefly in section III (7.27-30). Noticing the paucity of references to the Messiah in 4 Ezra, Michael Stone conjectured that the Messiah did not play a significant role in the author's purposes but had a significant role in his eschatological thought.[86] The previous analysis of the theodicy can confirm this insight. The author's purpose in the first four sections was to establish the validity of the eschatological answer to his problems, without which the eschatological speculations in sections V and VI would be meaningless.

Section VII

Section VII makes only brief mention of eschatolgical concepts. The periodization of history is mentioned to emphasize the closeness of the end (14.11-13). Judgment and resurrection are mentioned in connection with Ezra's final words of hope to the people. 'After death the judgment will come, when we shall live again; and the names of the righteous will become manifest, and the deeds of the ungodly will be disclosed'.[87]

E. *The Function of Eschatology*

The author of 4 Ezra attempted to provide hope to the Jewish people after the fall of Jerusalem in 70 CE. Building on the tradition of the prophets, the sinfulness of the people was the reason most often given for the misfortunes of the Jewish people. In light of this tradition, the fall of Jerusalem was only one more example of the perennial sinfulness of the people. This continual failure led the author of 4 Ezra to complain through the mouth of Ezra that God was unfair to hold Israel responsible when history showed that people were unable to refrain from sin. Through the angel the eschatological solution was offered to this problem. The chosen people's proven sinfulness, however, called this solution into question: How could a people unable to possess the promises due to their sinfulness hope to inherit the future world offered as the solution to their present distress? The eschatological solution could only be viable if the old problem of sin could be overcome. Ezra found the resolution of the sin problem in the mercy of God.[88] The mercy of God, however, would neither alleviate the present evils nor offer retribution to the righteous. The future hope was offered in 4 Ezra as the solution to this problem. In the future the righteous would receive their reward and the evil heart would be removed from the people and the nation would partake of the promises at last. Through the mercy of God, the Jewish people could look forward to the time when God's promises to Israel would be fulfilled.

Chapter 4

2 BARUCH

Second Baruch, or the Syriac Apocalypse of Baruch, is a Jewish work written after the fall of Jerusalem in 70 CE. The literary context, however, described the events as coming on the eve of and soon after the destruction of Jerusalem in 587 BCE. Baruch, Jeremiah's scribe, is the main character. The book consists of a series of dialogues between God and Baruch, the description of several visions which Baruch received from God, and the narration of conversations between Baruch and his people. It chronicles his struggle to understand the disaster which befell Jerusalem and his people, and his attempts to help the people understand this disaster.

The attempt to explain the evil which befell Jerusalem and the Jewish people has often been labeled a theodicy. Second Baruch narrates Baruch's movement from distress over the evil about to befall Jerusalem and the Jewish people, to an attitude of acceptance and consolation.[1] The chronicle of Baruch's changing attitude is intended to change the reader's attitude also. As Baruch struggles with the evil, the suffering, and the religious crisis caused by the destruction of Jerusalem, the reader is led to struggle with the religious problems which evil events can cause, and moved towards a change of attitude. Second Baruch thus can be considered a narrative theodicy.

This chapter will show that 2 Baruch is indeed a theodicy and delineate the function of eschatology in the theodicy. To accomplish this, it will briefly survey introductory matters, and then analyze the literary structure of 2 Baruch which provides the framework for the theodicy. The development of the theodicy will be traced and the eschatology sketched. Finally the function of the eschatology in the theodicy will be described.

A. *Introduction*

The study assumes the conclusions detailed in brief below regarding the best manuscripts, the original language, the date of composition, the provenance of the apocalypse, and the relationship of the letter to the apocalypse proper.

Manuscripts, Editions, and Translations

The entire manuscript of 2 Baruch is extant in only one Syriac manuscript (*Bibliotheca Ambrosiana*) from the sixth or seventh century.[2] Four short passages are known from Jacobite lectionaries.[3] An Arabic manuscript of chs. 3–77 has been discovered in the library of the Monastery of St. Catherine on Mount Sinai (Sinai No. 589).[4] A small fragment in Greek is known among the *Oxyrhynchus Papyri*, fragment no. 403.[5] The manuscript tradition of the letter (chs. 78–87) is different from that of the apocalypse proper, appearing most often separate from the apocalypse and found in at least thirty-six different Syriac texts.[6]

The major Syriac manuscript, *Bibliotheca Ambrosiana*, was first edited and published by A.M. Ceriani.[7] A second edition was published by M. Kmosko; this edition is rather uneven, however, since he freely emended the text and punctuation.[8] A modern edition of the apocalypse proper (chs. 1–77) is available in the *Old Testament in Syriac* series.[9] This edition was used as the text for this study.

R.H. Charles produced an annotated English translation of 2 Baruch which appeared in a slightly revised version in *Apocrypha and Pseudepigrapha of the Old Testament*.[10] P.M. Bogaert published a French translation with a full commentary.[11] A.F.J. Klijn has recently published both a new German and a new English translation.[12]

Original language

The heading of the Syriac text of 2 Baruch states that it is a translation of a Greek original. This is supported by the Greek fragments found among the *Oxyrhynchus Papyri*. The traditional view has held that the original language of 2 Baruch was Hebrew or at least Semitic.[13] P. Bogaert, however, after examining the arguments decided that they were not decisive. He left the door open for a possible Hebrew original, but did not consider it necessary.[14]

Date of Composition

A broad consensus places the date of composition of 2 Baruch somewhere between 70 and 132 CE. The exact date, however, is elusive. The *terminus a quo* of 2 Baruch is usually established by citation of passages such as 32.2-4 which presupposes two destructions of Jerusalem.

> For after a short time, the building of Zion will be shaken in order that it will be rebuilt. That building will not remain; but it will again be uprooted after some time and will remain desolate for a time. And after that it is necessary that it will be renewed in glory and that it will be perfected into eternity (2 Bar. 32.2-4).[15]

The *terminus ad quem* has proven to be much harder to establish. The various proposals are usually based on vague citations, either the relation of 2 Baruch to 4 Ezra or references to supposed historical events.[16] Most of the dating schemes place the *terminus ad quem* somewhere in the early to middle second century CE. None of the proposals, however, has succeeded in presenting a convincing argument for the exact determination of the *terminus ad quem.*

The Provenance

The author of 2 Baruch clearly took his stand with and addressed concerns of a Palestinian Jewish community. The ultimate destination, however, is not clear. Bogaert, building upon the evidence of the letter, identified the destination as the tribes of the diaspora.[17] The obvious Palestinian concerns with the reference to the diaspora tribes may suggest the work was intended to address all Judaism.[18]

The Letter

Chapters 78–87 of 2 Baruch comprise a letter written to the tribes of the diaspora mentioned in ch. 77. Previous scholarship has consistently considered this letter a part of 2 Baruch in spite of the differing manuscript tradition.[19] Bogaert, after examining the different manuscript traditions of the letter which either included it with the apocalypse proper or as a distinct unit, concluded that the differing traditions were a secondary phenomenon and did not require the letter to be separate. The judgment, therefore, about the connection between the letter and the apocalypse would have to be made on other grounds.[20] Bogaert's conclusion was based on the Syriac manuscript tradition; the recent discovery of a fairly complete Arabic manuscript (see above note 4) calls this conclusion into question. Konigsveld, after examining the Arabic document, concluded that the apocalypse and the letter were treated as two separate documents.[21] Bogaert, after examining the manuscript evidence, examined the similarities between the letter and the apocalypse, and concluded there was a fundamental unity between the two.[22] Gwendolyn Sayler also recently examined the connection between the letter and the apocalypse, and concluded on literary grounds that the letter is not a part of the apocalypse proper but an addition.[23] She listed the themes in the apocalypse which are lacking in the letter or used in a different manner, and differences of terminology between the two. On the basis of the differing manuscript traditions and the literary differences presented by Sayler, the separation of the letter and the apocalypse proper has been assumed in the following analysis. Second Baruch will refer in what follows to the apocalypse proper (chs. 1–77) and not the letter.

B. *Literary Structure*

It is assumed here that 2 Baruch was an organized theodicy designed to convince the reader that faith in the Lord was still a viable option in spite of the evils which had befallen the Jews. The methodology begins with the protagonist (Baruch) expressing the same doubts the reader might be experiencing and then moves the reader through the resolution of those doubts by the movement of Baruch through the resolution of his doubts.

Essential to an understanding of the argument is an understanding of the literary structure. The basic literary units are fairly easy to isolate—for example, narrative units, prayers, dialogues, etc.; the larger groupings and the overall structure have proven harder to isolate. Two recent studies have argued for the literary unity of 2 Baruch, and their analyses have helped to bring order and meaning out of this complex book.[24] The following analysis builds on the insight of these two studies, but with some modifications. In particular the flow and direction of the argument have contributed to the analysis presented here.

Second Baruch is a rather long and complex document comprised of numerous basic literary units joined by narrative sections. These basic literary units are easily isolated and grouped under categories.

These categories basically conform to standard form critical categories. The larger units and the overall structure, however, can only be isolated after an analysis of techniques used by the author in the composition of this work. Both Bogaert and Sayler have made suggestions about these techniques. These suggestions will be evaluated and expanded for this study.

The Basic Literary Units

The narrative's connecting links are easily isolated and have been recongnized by all who have given detailed study to 2 Baruch. They consist of narrative introductions (e.g. 1.1; 6.1-3), conclusions to larger units (e.g. 5.5-7; 9.1-2), and numerous short internal narrative links (e.g. 4.1; 5.1; 7.1). A major difficulty comes in separating the narrative conclusion of one section from the narrative introduction of the following section. Table 1 (p. 82) gives a graphic picture of some of the proposals for the overall structure and the grouping of the basic literary units of 2 Baruch, and illustrates the difficulty encountered in separating the narrative conclusions form the introductions. As shown in the first column, Renan and Schürer agreed on the literary analysis of 2 Baruch except for the break between the first and second sections, Renan placing the break at 12.5, and Schürer placing it at 12.4. A similar difficulty is encountered with the separation around chapter 47. This discrepancy is part of the overall problem of grouping the larger units and will be taken up again later.

A second group of basic literary units are speech units.[25] This group includes:

Laments by Baruch—10.6-12.4[26]; 35.1-4

Prayers by Baruch—21.4-25; 38.1-4; 48.2-24; 54.1-22

Dialogues between God and Baruch—1.2-5.4; 13.1-20.6; 22.1-30.5; 39.1-43.3; 48.26-52.7

A dialogue between Ramael and Baruch—55.4-76.4[27]

Speeches by Baruch—31.3-32.7; 44.2-45.2; 77.2-10

Conversations between Baruch and the people—32.8-34.1; 46.1-7; 77.11-17

Several observations about the function and setting of some of these basic units can help open up the structure. 1. Both laments were connected to a vision. The lament in chs. 10-12 followed and was a response to the preceding vision. The lament in ch. 35

Table 1

Proposed Literary Structures of 2 Baruch[a]

Schürer (Renan)	Violet	Bogaert	Sayler[b]	Proposed[c]
I 1.1–12.4 (1.1–12.5)	I 1.1–9.2	I 1.1–12.5	I 1.1–5.7	I 1.1–5.7
			II 6.1–20.6	II 6.1–9.2
	II 10.1–20.6			III 10.1–12.5
II 12.5–20.6 (13.1–20.6)		II 13.1–20.6		IV 13.1–21.1
III 21.1–34.1	III 21.1–34.1	III 21.1–34.1	III 21.1–30.5	V 21.2–34.1
			IV 31.1–43.3	
IV 35.1–46.7	IV 35.1–47.1	IV 35.1–47.1		VI 35.1–47.2
			V 44.1–52.8	
V 47.1–52.8	V 47.2–52.8	V 47.2–52.8		VII 48.1–77.26
VI 53.1–76.5	VI 53.1–76.5	VI 53.1–77.17	VI 53.1–76.5	
VII 77.1–87.1	VII 77.1–87.1		VII 77.1–77.26	
		VII 77.18–87.1		
				VIII ? 78.1–87.1

[a]The first three columns were adapted from Bogaert, *Apocalypse de Baruch*, I, p. 62.

[b]Sayler, *Have the Promises Failed?*

[c]Charles (*APOT*, I, pp. 481-504) presented basically the same outline; the only differences are at the precise verses for the breaks.

preceded the vision in ch. 36, which was a response to the lament. 2. The prayers can be subdivided. Two prayers (in chs. 21 and 48) prefaced a dialogue and set the parameters of the following dialogue. The other two prayers (in chs. 38 and 54) prefaced the interpretation of a vision and requested interpretation. 3. The speeches, much like the first type of prayer, prefaced a conversation with the people. These observations begin to show the probable outline of the larger grouping; for example, each prayer probably should be grouped with the following section.

The third group of basic literary units is visions. There were three visions: 6.4–8.2; 36.1–37.1; 53.1–12.[28]

The Larger Literary Units

The author of 2 Baruch grouped the basic literary units isolated above into larger units and into an overall structure. Bogaert identified four basic criteria by which the large literary units could be identified: (a) change of place; (b) a week of fasting; (c) the introduction of the people; (d) a certain autonomy of composition of the letter.[29] The criteria of Sayler were a little more general: (a) disparity between units; (b) inner coherence.[30]

A strict application of Bogaert's criteria yielded ten possible places in the document where units can be differentiated (see Table 2). In

Table 2

The Places Bogaert's Criteria Occur

	Change of Place	Fasts	People	Letter
1	5.5–6.1	5.7 (One day)	5.5-7 (Nobles)	
2	8.3–9.1	9.2	9.1-2 (Jeremiah)	
3		12.5		
4	21.1-2	21.1		
5	31.1		31.1–34.1 (Elders)	
6	35.1			
7	44.1		44.1–47.2 (Elders)	
8	47.1-2	47.2		
9	77.1		77.1-17 (All people)	
10	77.18			78.1

two places (5.5–6.1; 8.3–9.2—Rows 1 and 2) three criteria converged to signal the possible break: change of place, fasting, people.[31] In two locations (21.1-2; 47.1-2—Rows 4 and 8) a change of place and a fast converged to signal a possible break. In one place (12.5—Row 3) a fast alone signaled a possible break. In three locations (31.1–34.1; 44.1–47.2; 77.1-17—Rows 5, 7, 9) a change of place and the people signaled a possible break. The letter (77.18–78.1) signals the last possible break. A quick comparision of this data with the different proposed break points presented in Table 1 showed that only one proposed break (53.1) had none of Bogaert's criteria present to signal the break. A second point of note is that of the three places where a change of place and people converged, Sayler proposed breaks at all three, whereas the previous scholars proposed a break only at the last one (77.1).

Literary Analysis

Using the observations presented above, the following seven part structure can be detected. On the basis of parallel structure and subject matter, the book can also be divided at ch. 21 into two parallel halves. This structure is supported by numerous parallel structural and content elements, and also forms the integral framework of the argument. The following analysis of each of the seven parts justifies the proposed structure.

I. Introductory dialogue (1–5)
II. Vision 1 (6–9)
III. Lamentation (10–12)
IV. Dialogue 2 (13–21.1)

V. Dialogue 3 (21.2-34)
VI. Vision 2 (35–47)
VII. Vision 3 (48–77)

Section I. The first section (chs. 1–5) is composed of a narrative introduction, a dialogue between God and Baruch, and narrative conclusion. It can be outlined as follows:

A. Narrative introduction (1.1-2a)
B. Dialogue (1.2b–5.4)
C. Narrative conclusion (5.5-7)

The first section functions as the introduction to the whole book, establishing the setting, introducing the main characters, and presenting the main subjects.

The narrative introduction (1.1-2a) establishes the fictional setting of the book as the 'twenty-fifth year of Jeconiah, the king of Judah' and the identity of the main character as Baruch, the son of Neriah.

The dialogue between Baruch and the Lord (1.2b–5.4) introduces the problem and then raises the issues which occupy the rest of the book. The problem is the announced destruction of Jerusalem, and the issues raised by this announcement are : (1) the fate of the Jewish nation, and (2) the justness of God who punished the Jews, while letting the nations who deny God go unpunished. After Baruch hears of the coming destruction, he first wishes for death, and then, through a series of objections, questions the fairness of God. All of Baruch's objections boil down to one major concern: If Jerusalem is destroyed, what will happen to the Jewish nation?[32] The Lord assures Baruch that the destruction of the earthly Jerusalem is not the end, since the destruction is only for a time, and the *real* Jerusalem is in heaven (4.1-7). Baruch once more objects, this time by complaining that the enemies will boast over their victory while the Jewish nation suffers (5.1). The Lord answers by saying not to worry about his name and glory but about his judgment, by emphasizing that he and not the enemy will overthrow Jerusalem (5.2-4). Baruch's questioning God's justness in relationship to the fate of the Jewish nation, and the demand for judgment upon the enemies, dominates the rest of the book.

The narrative conclusion (5.5-7) signals the end of the section through Baruch's exit to the valley of Kidron, the mention of the people, and the fast in 5.5. The pattern which this conclusion presents forms the basic framework for all the conclusions. This pattern is the change of place, the introduction of the people, and the fast. This framework is supported by its repeated use, with slight variations, throughout the book.

The elements comprising this framework were listed above as the first three criteria of Bogaert, and are the only ones which can apply here. Bogaert, however, failed even to mention the convergence of the three criteria here when outlining the plan of 2 Baruch.[33] Charles placed the break between the first two sections just before the fast (5.6) as he consistently did with all the others.[34] Charles's reasoning for this seems to be based on his assumption that all the fasts were preparation for a coming revelation.[35] The first fast, however, clearly responded to the destruction of Jerusalem; the second fast responded to the vision of the destruction (9.1) and was followed by a lament; the third fast (12.5) continued the mood set by the preceding lament. Only the last two fasts clearly prepared for revelation, and in both instances Baruch was commanded to fast by the Lord (see 20.5-6; 43.3). The outline proposed here, therefore, places the breaks after the fasts, since the first three were clearly related to the preceding material.[36] The fasts served the function not only of dividing the sections but also of linking them together. This double function caused much of the disagreement about their placement.

Section II. The second section (chs. 6–9) consists of a narrative introduction, a vision, and a narrative conclusion. It can be outlined as follows:

A. Narrative introduction (6.1-3)
B. Vision (6.4-8.2)
C. Narrative conclusion (8.3–9.2)

The narrative introduction (6.1-3) tells how the army comes and surrounds the city. As a result, Baruch goes outside to mourn and while outside is caught up by a strong spirit.

The vision (6.4–8.2) describes how the angels overthrow the city and take the vessels from the temple and hide them in the earth for safe keeping, fulfilling what the Lord promised Baruch in 4.3: the enemy would not overthrow the city but the Lord would. Baruch's two concerns, the continuance of the Jewish nation and anger against the enemy, are symbolically addressed in this vision. The angels take the vessels out of the temple and hide them in the earth until the temple's restoration in the last times, showing there is a future for the Jewish nation. Since the angels destroy the city walls and let the enemy in, the enemy's boasting is quelled. This connects the vision to the first section; it is a fullfillment of the things the Lord told Baruch would happen. This section is also connected the following section, since the fulfillment of the judgment upon Jerusalem prompts the following lament. The connections in subject matter and content between the first three sections are probably what made Bogaert go against his criteria and end the first section at 12.5.[37] The obvious connection between the announcement of the destruction of

Jerusalem in section I and the fulfillment of it in the vision of section II make it hard to separate the vision from the first section, as Sayler did, in light of her criteria of disparity and inner coherence. According to Sayler's criterion of inner coherence, the first three sections should be included all in one section as Bogaert did.[38] Thus in the absence of other criteria, a strong case could be made for the unity of 1.1–20.6 on the basis of common subject matter and theme. The breaks proposed here between the sections in this first half were made primarily on the basis of the criteria isolated by Bogaert. The unity of content and theme among the first three sections can be explained on the basis of the division into halves. This uniformity in structure among the first three sections supports the division into halves.

The narrative conclusion (8.3–9.2) tells how the Babylonian army come in and take the city. The end of the section is signaled by Baruch's leaving (8.3), joining with Jeremiah and fasting for seven days (9.1-2). Once again the pattern in the conclusion is the departure of Baruch, the introduction of other people (in this case Jeremiah), and the seven-day fast. Again, in contrast to Charles, the fast is clearly a response to the destruction of Jerusalem just described. The fast was a fast of mourning and not an ascetic exercise in preparation for a revelation: 'we rent our garments, and wept and mourned, and fasted seven days'.[39]

Section III. Section III (chs. 10–12) consists of a narrative introduction, a lament, and a narrative conclusion.

A.	Narrative introduction (10.1-5)
B.	Lamentation (10.6–12.4)
C.	Narrative conclusion (12.5)

The narrative introduction (10.1-5) relates how, after the seven-day fast, the word of the Lord comes to Baruch. Baruch is instructed to tell Jeremiah to go to Babylon, while remaining in Jerusalem himself to receive further revelations.

The lament (10.6–12.4) refects the two sides of Baruch's reaction to the fall of Jerusalem. In the first half of the lament, Baruch expresses his grief over the loss of Jerusalem, and in the second half he expresses his anger against Babylon. This two-sided reaction parallels Baruch's reaction to the announcement of the coming judgment in ch. 3. Baruch's initial reaction in ch. 3 to the destruction of Jerusalem shows concern about the survival of the Jewish nation. The lament, in much the same tones, spoke of the despair the destuction of Jerusalem brought. Further, both Baruch's initial reaction in section I (3.2) and the lament in this section (10.6) begin with a death wish. Baruch's second concern in the first section is with the enemies' boasting (5.1). Likewise, the lament here is followed by Baruch's reaction to the boasting of Babylon over the destruction of Jerusalem, in chs. 11 and 12. Note that ch. 12 already shows a movement of Baruch away from the total despair expressed in the first section, by his announcement to Babylon that her joy would only last a little while; then judgment would fall upon her.

In the narrative conclusion (12.5) Baruch fasted for seven days. The fast is the only clear indicator of the break between this and the next section, but a fast was the only common indicator of a break within the first half. Sayler argued against Bogaert's ending his first section here. She listed two criticisms. First, she pointed out the connection between the lament and the following dialogue (chs. 13–20), particulary citing the 'prosperity motif'.[40] She failed, however, to note the connection between the boasting of the enemies in the first section (5.1) and the complaint about the prosperity of the nations here. Second, and integral to her analysis, she argued that ch. 12 was not part of the lament. Her basis for separating ch. 12 from the rest of the lament was the bracketing of 10.5–11.7 by death wishes at the beginning and the end of this section (10.5-6; 11.6-7). She also pointed out that ch. 12 moves beyond the lament by expressing the belief that judgment would fall upon Babylon. Chapter 12, however, serves the almost obligatory function of the statement of trust in God at the end of a lament. The movement to trust and hope, or in this case assurance of judgment upon the enemies, is a regular part of a lament. She also failed to recognize the connection between the wish for death in section I, and the wish for death in the lament as pointed out above.

Section IV. The fourth section (13.1–21.1) consists of a narrative introduction, a dialogue between God and Baruch, and a narrative conclusion.

A. Narrative introduction (13.1)
B. Dialogue (13.2–20.6)
C. Narrative conclusion (21.1)

The narrative introduction (13.1) placed Baruch on Mount Zion where the word of the Lord came to him. This was the last time in 2 Baruch a divine communication to Baruch was called 'the word' of God.[41] The occurrence of this phrase at two of the three break points (10.1; 13.2) in the first half strengthens these breaks. The absence of the phrase to introduce a divine communication in the second half of the book further supports the division into halves.

The dialogue (13.2–20.6) continues the discussion about the dual concerns of the fate of the Jewish nation and the enemies. Once again, the Lord initiates the conversation with Baruch. Like the previous section, except in reverse order, the dialogue has two parts: the first about the enemies, the second about the Jews. After a brief discussion about the coming judgment upon the enemies, the conversation changes direction. Baruch asks about the fate of the righteous. His questions about the righteous can be boiled down into one real concern: in light of the destruction of Jerusalem, what did it profit one to be righteous, since the righteous as well as the wicked were punished? The resulting discussion about the fate of the righteous marks a subtle shift in the argument. The conversation has begun to turn from a concern about the nation to a concern about the righteous few within the nation. Note also that for the first time Baruch is commanded to fast (20.5) in preparation for further revelations.

The narrative conclusion (21.1) tells how Baruch fasted seven days as commanded. The end of the section is signaled once again by a change of place and a seven-day fast. The reasoning for labeling 21.1 as the conclusion is the mention of Baruch going away and fasting for seven days, as in the preceding conclusions. Further, 21.2 begins like the preceding introduction, telling how Baruch comes back to the temple.

Several characteristic features and concerns are repeated throughout the first half of the book (sections I–IV). 1. Each of the sections is composed of a narrative introduction, one middle section and a narrative conclusion. 2. The Lord initiates the contracts in each section. Three times the word comes to Baruch (1.1; 10.1; 13.2). 3. Baruch's major concern in the first half is with the nation, whereas his concern in the second half is the faithful few. 4. The discussions always center upon God's fairness or justice in bringing the judgment upon the city and the people. 5. The people are always mentioned in a narrative context. These similarities in structure and content among the first four sections support the outline proposed here.[42]

Section V. The structure of section V (21.2–34.1) signals a clear break from the preceding sections. This section is composed of a narrative introduction, a prayer by Baruch, a dialogue between Baruch and the Lord, a speech to the people, and a conversation with the people. It can be outlined as follows:

A. Narrative introduction (21.2-3)
B. Prayer (21.4-25)
C. Dialogue (21.26–30.5)
D. Speech to the people (31.1–32.7)
E. Conversation with the people (32.8–34.1)

The narrative introduction (21.2-3) places Baruch back where the Lord has previously spoken to him.

The prayer by Baruch (21.4-25) outlines the new perspective and new concerns which occupy the latter half of the book. It begins with an affirmation of the greatness of God (vv. 4-11) and the certainty of the afterlife (vv. 12-18). Baruch then asks the questions which will dominate the rest of the book. He first asks when the glorious future will happen, and second, when the enemies will be judged. The prayer closes with a request for God to hasten the time of the end. Characteristic of the three sections in the last half of Baruch is the opening of the section with a prayer by Baruch (see also 35.2-4; 48.1-25). In contrast to the sections in the first half, Baruch is the initiator of the contact.

The resulting dialogue (21.26–30.5) centers on the future. The Lord first replies that the promises about the future will happen (22.1–24.2), and the nations will be judged. Baruch asks for more information about what will happen to the enemies and when it will happen (24.3-4). The discussion turns to the tribulation and the ensuing terrors.

Baruch then goes to the people and exhorts them (31.1–32.7) to follow the law, warning them of the coming evils and encouraging them about their future glories.

Sayler parted company with previous scholarship at this point by separating Baruch's interaction with the people (31.1–34.1) from the preceding dialogue,[43] and using it as the beginning of the next section

(35.1 ff.). Her criteria were the changes of place and characters, and the unity of issues and themes throughout 21.1–30.5. She did not give the same weight, however, to the change of place, characters, and issues at 35.1.[44] Previously, the change of place and characters occurred at the point where Baruch went to encounter the Lord, and there is no indication that anything different happened here. Using the criteria of change of place and character and by analogy with previous sections, the next section should begin with 35.1 and not 31.1, as Sayler contended.[45] Since the speech to the people brings the message Baruch has just received, it should be connected with this preceding dialogue. Further, the conclusions of sections I and II (5.5-7; 8.3–9.2) have a structure analogous to 31.1–34.1. Both of these previous conclusions included Baruch's going to the people. This concluding section would seem only an expansion. Further, the lament (35.2-4) parallels the introductory prayers of sections V and VII (21.4-25; 48.1-25).

In the first half Baruch had doubts about the goodness of God and worried about the future but now these doubts and worries are allayed. In the second half the people express much the same doubts and worries which Baruch expressed in the first. A literary parallel exists between Baruch's doubts in the first half and the people's in the second half. When Baruch begins to leave after talking with the people, they stop him and beg him not to leave (32.8–34.1). They speak to him in much the same tones about their survival if he should leave as he earlier spoke to God about the survival of the nation if Jerusalem should fall.[46]

Section VI. The structure of section VI (chs. 35–47) is similar to the preceding section. It consists of a narrative introduction, a lament, a vision, a request for interpretation of the vision, a dialogue concerning the interpretation, a speech to the people, a conversation with the people, and a narrative conclusion.

A. Narrative introduction (35.1)
B. Lamentation (35.2-4)
C. Vision (36.1–37.1)
D. Prayer for interpretation (38.1-4)
E. Dialogue about interpretation (39.1–43.3)
F. Speech to the people (44.1–45.2)
G. Conversation with people (46.1-7)
H. Narrative conclusion (47.1-2)

The section begins (35.1) with Baruch at the ruins of the holy place lamenting the nation's fate. In the lament (35.2-4), as in the prayer at the beginning of the preceding section, Baruch initiates the contact and is the first participant. The lament is a response to the destruction of the temple.

The vision (36.1–37.1) appears as a response to Baruch's lament over the destruction of the temple, and is meant to offer some comfort. In direct contrast to the relationship of the lament and the vision in the first half, the vision is a response to the lament; in the first half (6.1–12.5), the vision prompts the lament. This difference marks the changed attitude of Baruch in the second half as compared to the first.

Baruch immediately prays for the interpretation of the vision, (38.1-4) claiming that he has always been associated with the law and the Lord's wisdom.

The dialogue concerning the interpretation of the vision (39.1–43.1) begins with an interpretation, which centers mainly upon the Messiah and his victory. Baruch responds by asking two questions. 1. To whom would these things happen? 2. What about your people who have abandoned their faith and those who have returned to their faith? The Lord tells Baruch that good things will come to the faithful and evil things to the wicked. The last state of the person will determine his final state. Baruch is assured that he personally will be taken.

Sayler pointed out the shift in Baruch's questions at this point.[47] Baruch's concern had now shifted from the nation as a whole to two groups within the nation: those Jews who no longer follow the Torah, and the faithful Jews and proselytes. This shift further highlighted the differences between the first and second halves.

After receiving the vision and its interpretation, Baruch leaves to speak to the people (44.1–45.2).[48] He encourages them to follow the law and commandments, and promises that if they endure and persevere they will participate in the consolation of Zion. He exhorts them to look to the future and the period which will remain forever. Notice how Baruch's words of consolation also answer his previous lament.

The people then express their concern that Baruch will leave them (46.1-7). He assures them they will always have a leader. Once again, the reaction of the people to the departure of Baruch parallels his reaction to the destruction of Jerusalem in the first half.

The narrative conclusion places Baruch back at the temple where he fasts seven days as commanded earlier. Baruch's speech and conversation with the people is bracketed by the instruction to fast and the actual fast, suggesting that 44.1–46.7 is the conclusion to section VI rather than the introduction to the following section.[49] The end of the section is signaled by a change of place (47.1), a fast (47.2), and a change of characters (47.1–48.1).

Section VII. Section VII (chs. 48–77) again had a structure similar to the preceding section. It is composed of a narrative introduction, a prayer, a dialogue between Baruch and the Lord, a vision, a request for interpretation of the vision, a dialogue about the interpretation, a speech to the people, a conversation with the people, and a narrative conclusion.

A.	Narrative introduction (48.1)
B.	Prayer (48.2-25)
C.	Dialogue (48.26–52.7)
D.	Vision (53.1-12)
E.	Prayer for interpretation (54.1-22)
F.	Dialogue about interpretation (55.1–76.4)
G.	Speech to people (77.1-10)
H.	Conversation with people (77.11-17)
I.	Narrative conclusion (77.18-26)

The narrative introduction (48.1) simply introduces the prayer; Baruch is already in the place where the Lord has spoken to him. In the prayer (48.2-25), Baruch's intercession for the people, he affirms that the Lord is master of the times and powers, and asks for help for those who submit to him and deliverance from judgment. Baruch's changed concern for the faithful among the Jews, and not the whole nation, is evident here. Once again, as throughout the second half, Baruch initiates the contact with the Lord.

The following dialogue (48.26–52.7) is initially a response to the prayer. The Lord answers Baruch that the people will be dealt with according to their deeds. The conversation quickly turns to the fate of the righteous and the shape of their resurrection bodies. Baruch laments the destruction of the wicked and exhorts the righteous to enjoy their suffering. Sayler listed several statements in this dialogue which parallel and reverse Baruch's statements in section I, and show the change in Baruch's attitude.

> He replaces his early query '... if You deliver Your people to those who *hate* us ...' (3.5) with an exhortation to the righteous to rejoice in present suffering rather than paying attention to the deviation of those who *hate* them (52.6). He substitutes the confident assertion '... I will not be silent in celebrating the *praise* kept for the righteous...' (48.49) for the initial question '... how shall we speak Your *praise*? ...' (3.6). He answers his question '... will the world return to its nature and the age depart to primeval silence? ...' (3.7) by affirming that this world is moving toward a final judgment in which the righteous will be given the world to come (48.45-50; 52.1-7).[50]

Sayler, agreeing with Bogaert and other scholars, except Charles, called the dialogue the end of the section. All scholars admit, however, that this is the most difficult break to ascertain. The only clear indication of the break, according to Bogaert, is the differing subject matter of the dialogue which centers on the resurrection, and the vision and its interpretation which present a historical overview.[51] Those who ended this section with ch. 52 on the basis of differing content have not paid close attention to the relation of these two themes in the preceding sections. The dialogue in section V (21.26–30.5) contained both a historical overview (27.1–28.2) and a discussion about the resurrection (30.2-5). Likewise, the vision and its interpretation in section VI (36.1–43.3) also contain a historical overview (39.1–40.4) and a section on the resurrection (42.7-8).

The vision (53.1-12) of a series of black and bright waters or clouds shows no signs of a break with the previous dialogue, such as a change of place or fast.

After the vision is given Baruch prays for its interpretation (54.1-22). In this prayer he affirms that a man's deeds determine his destiny, with even Adam causing only his own death.

The ensuing dialogue between Baruch and Ramael about the interpretation (55.1–76.4) concerns twelve series of black and bright waters followed by a pair of final waters, all of which represent ages upon the earth. Baruch is finally instructed to go tell the people what he has learned (77.1-10). In his speech to the people, he exhorts them to follow the law so that the Lord will be merciful to them.[52]

The people respond to Baruch by asking him to write a letter of encouragement to the people in Babylon (77.11-17). He replies that he will write to those in Babylon and those of the diaspora.

The narrative conclusion (77.18-26) tells how Baruch writes the two letters, one to be sent by three men to Babylon and the other by an eagle to the nine-and-a-half other tribes.

Bogaert began his last section, which included the letter, with 77.18. Indications of a break would be the change of place and time indication. This short narrative section is not complete enough to stand on its own. Since it has been argued here that the letter does not belong with the book, this narrative section should be considered the conclusion of the last section and also of the book.

As with the first half, the second half shows a unity of structure and content supporting the proposed division. Each of the three sections in the second half begins with Baruch initiating the contact by either a prayer, or in one case, a lament (21.4-25; 35.2-4; 48.1-25); this contrasts with the first half where God initiates all the contacts. The three sections in the second half show a certain structural symmetry. Section V features a dialogue with God as its centerpiece. Section VI has a vision followed by a dialogue about its interpretation. Section VII has both a dialogue and a vision followed by a dialogue about its interpretation. Each section has a historical overview and speaks of the resurrection. Finally, each section ends with Baruch going to the people.

C. *Theodicy*

Second Baruch traces the crisis of faith caused by the destruction of Jerusalem in 70 CE. This crisis was presented as the crisis of the book's main character Baruch. As a result of the crisis in his life, Baruch questions some of the basic tenets of his faith. This crisis is intensified because God has not only allowed this great evil to happen; he has initiated it. The narration of Baruch's attempt to reconcile his belief in a benevolent God while Jerusalem is subjected to a pagan and evil nation constitutes the theodicy.

The destruction of Jerusalem caused Baruch to question the justness of God, and as was seen in the earlier analysis, this questioning is reflected in two major concerns addressed by him. 1. He questions the justness of God in bringing judgment upon Israel, since Israel was God's chosen. 2. As the corollary of this concern, he questions why the nations were not also judged. Tracing these two overarching concerns throughout 2 Baruch will open up the theodicy.

The major break between chs. 21 and 22 found in the analysis of the structure is the major break for the argument also. In the first half, God convinces Baruch of the justness of his actions in bringing destruction upon Jerusalem, and in the second half Baruch convinces the people of the justness of God's actions. In the first half the justice of God occupies most of the discussion but in the second half the guilt of the people occupies center stage. Baruch's concern about the continuation of the Jewish nation in the first half is answered in the second half with the promise of resurrection. Baruch's concern about judgment upon the nations in the first half is answered by the historical overviews in the second half emphasizing the certainty of judgment.

God's Judgment upon Israel

Baruch's initial reaction to the announcement of the coming destruction of Jerusalem because of the sins of the Jewish people is an attempt to switch the guilt from the people to God. He accuses God of abandoning his people to evil and forgetting his promises to Moses. The first half of the book is dedicated to proving that God is not guilty of the charges brought against him. When Baruch becomes convinced of the justness of God's actions late in the first half, he turns in the second half to the guilt of the people and the glorious future promised to the righteous.

Section I. The first section introduces the disaster which gave rise to Baruch's crisis of faith. Upon hearing of the coming destruction, Baruch questions God.

> What will happen after these things? For if you destroy your city and deliver up your country to those who hate us, how will the name of Israel be remembered again? Or how shall we speak again about your glorious deeds? Or to whom again will that which is in your Law be explained? Or will the universe return to its nature and the world go back to its original silence? And will the multitude of the souls be taken away and will not the nature of man be mentioned again? And where is all that which you said to Moses about us? (2 Bar. 3.4b-9)

The reason initially given for the destruction of Jerusalem was the sins of the people. These questions, however, were questions about the integrity of God and his promises to the Jewish nation, and did not relate to the sins of the people. Baruch was thus attempting to switch the guilt from man to God. In this area 2 Baruch is a true theodicy for it attempts to justify the actions of God in the face of evil. God initially answers Baruch's accusations by telling him that the destruction of Jerusalem is only temporary, thereby implying a future for the Jewish nation. God further replies that the real Jerusalem is in heaven, implying thereby that all the promises will remain intact since the real Jerusalem will remain intact.

Section II. The vision of the second section illustrated the initial answer which God gave Baruch concerning Jerusalem. In the vision, Baruch sees God's angels coming to remove the holy objects from the Holy of Holies and to hide them in the earth until the restoration of Jerusalem, further emphasizing that the destruction of Jerusalem does not signal the end of the Jewish nation.

Section III. Baruch's lament in section III once again echoes the concerns he raised in section I as a result of the destruction of Jerusalem. In the first half of the lament (10.6-19), Baruch expresses his grief over the destruction of Jerusalem by pronouncing a woe upon the living and almost everything else which brings happiness.

> Blessed is he who was not born,
>   or he who was born and died.
> But we, the living, woe to us,
>   because we have seen those afflictions of Zion,
>   and that which has befallen Jerusalem (2 Bar. 10.6-7).

This part of the lament does not address the intellectual problem of the continuance of the Jewish nation which the destruction raised for Baruch but a crisis of spirit. Notice how no accusations are made and no excuses offered. The lament expresses the despair Baruch has experienced in the face of evil, and functions within the theodicy as an expression of the spiritual problem the theodicy addresses. This indicates that 2 Baruch is meant not only to give intellectual solace and understanding, when confronting the problem of evil, but also to bring hope and uplift the spirit.

Section IV. This section begins with a discussion of the coming judgment of the wicked but quickly turns from this to focus mainly on the present plight of the righteous. Baruch wonders what good it has done for the righteous to be righteous (14.2-7). As with all of ch. 14, it is important here to ascertain of whom Baruch is speaking. The righteous spoken of here are the righteous among the Jews, for Baruch later complains that their righteousness should have saved the nation. One also needs to be aware that this passage concerns the present fortunes of the righteous and not their eschatological destiny. Baruch clearly expresses the eschatological hope later in the argument.

> For the righteous justly have good hope for the end and go away from this habitation without fear because they possess with you a store of good works which is preserved in treasuries. Therefore, they leave this world without fear and are confident of the world which you have promised to them with an expectation full of joy (2 Bar. 14.12-13).

His complaint echoed the old complaint that the wicked prosper and the righteous perish, with a change. He complained that even though the wicked will be punished in the end, most of the wicked have departed in happiness, so that when the tribulation comes few will be left to punish.

> I know there are many who have sinned and who have lived in happiness and who have left the world, but there will be few nations left in those times to which those words can be spoken which you said (2 Bar. 14.2).

The righteous Jews, on the other hand, were punished along with the rest of the nation because of the sins of the unrighteous. Surely the nation deserved to be forgiven because of the righteous as well as punished because of the wicked.

> What have they profited who have knowledge before you, and who did not walk in vanity like the rest of the nations, and who did not say to the dead: 'Give life to us', but always feared you and did not leave your ways? And, behold, they have been diligent and, nevertheless, you had no mercy on Zion on their account. And if there are others who did evil, Zion should have been forgiven on account of the works of those who did good works and should not have been overwhelmed because of the works of those who acted unrighteously (2 Bar. 14.5-7).

Here Baruch struggles with individual versus collective retribution. It is evident from the opening question of this passage that he is really concerned with why the righteous suffer and not why the Jewish nation was punished. He cannot understand why the righteous have had to suffer for the sins of the wicked. If he were concerned with the fate of the nation, then he should have been satisfied by the previous pronouncement that the Jewish nation was punished first in order that they might be forgiven (13.10). This is the first indication of Baruch's shifting concern from the Jewish nation as a whole to the righteous within the Jewish nation.

Baruch continues his complaint by charging that God's judgment is beyond human comprehension, implying thereby that God was not just in bringing judgment upon humanity (14.8-12). He acknowledges the future blessedness of the righteous but complains about the present evils and those yet to come. As with the previous passage, Baruch seems concerned only with the righteous among the Jews. The heart of his complaint is that many righteous have died and passed on to glory and have not had to experience suffering like him and those like him.

> Woe to those of us who have also now been treated shamefully and who await evils at that time. But you know exactly what you have made of your servants, for we are not able to understand that which is good like you, our Creator (2 Bar. 14.14-15).

Baruch charges God with acting unfairly to his generation in comparison with previous generations. Compare Baruch's lament in chs. 10 to 12.

> Blessed is he who was not born,
> or he who was born, and died.
> But we, the living, woe to us . . . (2 Bar. 10.6-7).

> O Lord, how have you born it? Our fathers went to rest without grief and, behold, the righteous sleep at rest in the earth. For they did not know this anguish nor did they hear that which has befallen us (2 Bar. 11.4-5).

Baruch concludes his plea by complaining that the world which was made for humanity remains, while the people for whom it was made are destroyed (14.17-19), thereby echoing one of his initial questions (3.7). Once again Baruch complains about the present fortunes of the righteous, this time implying that it is unfair that the righteous should suffer and die in the midst of a world which they should be enjoying.

Baruch's concern throughout this passage is mainly with the Jewish nation and specifically with the righteous among the Jewish people. He no longer complains about the unfairness of God punishing the Jewish nation but about the unfairness of the suffering the righteous have to endure.

The answer Baruch receives to his complaint, however, does not reflect many of Baruch's specific complaints, but instead points him to the eschaton. He receives a two-part answer addressing first God's dealings with the wicked and then those with the righteous. Once again it is necessary to be clear to whom the passage refers. Here it must be the Jewish nation, for it is they who have received the law, and the judgment upon the Jewish nation is Baruch's main concern. God defends his judgement upon the wicked Jews by making reference to the law.

> It is true that man would not have understood my judgment if he had not received the Law and if he were not instructed with understanding. But now because he trespassed, having understanding, he will be punished because he has understanding (2 Bar. 15.5-6).

The righteous, however, are to take no account of this world and the evils which they endure, but instead are to look to the world to come, which will be a crown with great glory (15.7-8). And so Baruch's complaints about the unfairness of the righteous suffering for the sins of the wicked are dismissed. The wicked deserve to be punished and the righteous are not to be concerned with this world but with the next.

Baruch, however, is still not convinced, and complains of the difficulty of inheriting eternity in the short time alloted man (16.1). The Lord answers Baruch that time is not the important factor, but obedience to the law of Moses (17.1-4). Baruch objects to this answer by pointing out how only a few followed Moses, but many followed Adam. God denied any responsibility for this by mentioning the covenant which accompanied the giving of the law to Moses; those who knowingly transgressed the covenant deserved what they got. Baruch is further exhorted not to think about all this, but instead to think about what glory awaits him in the near future. Baruch is then told that the destruction of Zion, which included the suffering of the righteous, even hastened the advent of the glorious future (20.2).

The complaints raised by Baruch and the answers given in this section marked a turning point in the argument. Up to and including this passage, Baruch has identified the fortunes of the righteous with the fortunes of the nation. This identification was the basis for part of his complaint. The answers which he receives, however, make a clear distinction between the fortunes of the wicked and those of the righteous, even within Israel.[53]

Section V. As pointed out in the analysis of the structure of 2 Baruch, the structure of this section departs from the structure of the previous sections and marks a turning point in the argument. Baruch is the first actor in this section, initiating the contact with God, and setting the agenda for the ensuing dialogue. The nature and subject matter of Baruch's meetings with God change, and Baruch's conversations with the people play an important role.

The section begins with Baruch's prayer, introduced by an affirmation of the greatness of God and the certainty of the afterlife.

> You know where you have preserved the end of those who have sinned or the fulfillment of those who have proved themselves to be righteous. For if only this life exists which everyone possesses here, nothing could be more bitter than this (2 Bar. 21.12-13).

He then asks the question which occupies most of the rest of the book.

> How long will corruption remain, and until when will the time of mortals be happy, and until when will those who pass away be polluted by the great wickedness in this world? (2 Bar. 21.19).

Now Baruch prays that the end will hasten and that God will bring about the promised times.

This prayer represents a different attitude for Baruch. No longer does he complain and accuse God of unfairness in his dealings with the Jewish nation or even the righteous among the Jews. He instead affirms the afterlife when the wicked will receive their end and the righteous their fulfillment. He insists that the afterlife is a necessity since this life is so bitter. No longer does he question God about the destruction of Jerusalem and its implications, but he asks him about what will happen in the future and pleads for this future to hasten.

In answer to Baruch's questions, the Lord replies first with a series of rhetorical questions which emphasize that the end is coming.

> Who starts on a journey and does not complete it? Or who will be comforted making a sea voyage unless he can reach a harbor? (2 Bar. 22.3).

Baruch is then told that when Adam sinned and death entered, the number of souls who would be born was determined (23.40). He is further told that the time of the end is drawing closer. All of these replies seem designed to offer assurance and comfort: assurance that the present evil time will end and comfort that the end is close. This attempt to offer hope and comfort, through the assurance of the reality of the future and the ever increasing completeness of the description of the future in the second half, represents not a rational attempt at theodicy, but an irrational attempt. The increasing complexity and completeness of the description of the future add no new rational dimentions to the discussion, but instead answer the crisis in spirit detailed in the first half of the lament in ch. 10.

After a vision of the coming judgment, Baruch goes to the people and calls the elders together. He warns them that worse suffering is coming, and exhorts them not to mourn about the present as a result. If they will follow the law, they will be protected by God in that time. Baruch's exhortation to the people reflects the previous dialogues; the present sufferings are downplayed and the guilt is placed upon the people; the salvation of the nation is not addressed, only the salvation of the individual.

This section marks a significant change in the tone of the book. Baruch no longer questions and accuses God concerning the fall of Jerusalem. For the first time he goes to the people, not only to exhort them, but also to offer them hope. At this point it would seem that Baruch's religious crisis is over, although the people are having problems and require convincing by Baruch. They cannot imagine going on without him to lead them, just as earlier he could not imagine the loss of Jerusalem.

Section VI. Baruch once again opens the section, this time with a lament (ch. 35). As in the section before, however, he does not question God about his actions or accuse him of unfairness. Unlike his reaction in the first lament (chs. 10–12), Baruch does not wish for death or otherwise bemoan this life; he simply expresses grief over the destruction of Jerusalem. This difference further emphasizes the change in him. His prayer after receiving a vision (ch. 38) likewise reflects his changed attitude. He expresses his devotion to God's law and asks for the interpretation of the vision. Since he no longer questions God's justness and fairness, it could be supposed that he has changed directions and become more concerned about the esoteric knowledge of future things than about the problems which the destruction of Jerusalem caused him. Even though he no longer questions God's justness or fairness, however, the vision in this section is given in response to his lament over the fall of Jerusalem, and serves to bring hope about the future. Further, both the ensuing dialogue concerning the vision and its interpretation, and his speech to the people deal with issues of theodicy.

Baruch receives a vision which describes the rise and fall of kingdoms. The ensuing discussion about the vision and its interpretation, however, departs from the content of the vision. He does not ask about the vision, but about those worthy to experience the events mentioned in the vision. He specifically mentions proselytes to the Jewish faith and Jews who have turned from the faith. God tells him that good things will happen to those who believe and evil things to those who do not believe. Concerning the proselytes and apostates, he is told that their latter state would determine their destiny: proselytes will experience the good, but the unfaithful Jews will experience evil. Continuing the direction established in ch. 14, a distinction is made between the fortunes of the Jewish nation and the fortunes of the righteous few within the nation. The Jewish nation is not even mentioned as the benefactor of the good which will come in the Messianic era; rather it is those, both Jew and proselyte, who follow the law and are careful to obey its statutes. This change of perspective relates directly to the question first raised by Baruch in ch. 3. 'Where is all that which you said to Moses about us?'[54] The righteous would receive the fulfillment of the promises, and not the nation.

Baruch's speech to the people emphasizes the themes found in the previous vision and dialogue. He emphasizes that God is just, and the present suffering is nothing compared with the future glory. This world is transitory and will be forgotten, but the world to come will not pass away. Those who follow the law will inherit the future.

Once again, little new is added, other than further descriptions of the future life and the conditions for entering. The only pure theodicy statements are Baruch's comments to the people about the justness of God's actions. The description of the future life, however, strengthened hope in the future and gave more credibility to the irrational theodicy which projected retribution into the future.

Section VII. This section likewise begins with a prayer of Baruch.

It joins together the two major themes found throughout the book: the fate of the righteous and judgment upon the enemies. Baruch affirms that God is the Lord and Determiner of history.

> O Lord, you summon the coming of the times,
> and they stand before you.
> You cause the display of power of the worlds to pass away
> and they do not resist you.
> You arrange the course of the periods,
> and they obey you.
> Only you know the length of the generations,
> and you do not reveal your secrets to many (2 Bar. 48.2-3).

He complains about the judgment which God has brought upon the righteous Jews and asks for relief.

> For behold, by your gift we come into the world,
> and we do go not of our own will.
> For we did not say to our parents: 'Begat us',
> nor have we sent to the realm of death saying: 'Receive us'.
> What therefore is our strength that we can bear you wrath,
> or what are we that we can endure your judgment?
> Protect us in your grace,
> and in your mercy help us (2 Bar. 48.15-18).

The distinction noted above between the nation and the righteous is further emphasized here. The righteous are now described with those characteristics used earlier to describe the nation.[55]

> For these are the people whom you have elected,
> and this is the nation of which you found no equal.
> In you we have put our trust,
> because, behold, your law is with us,
> and we know that we do not fall
> as long as we keep your statutes.
> We shall always be blessed;
> at least, we did not mingle with the nations.
> For we are all a people of the Name;
> we, who received one Law from the One.
> And that law that is among us will help us,
> and that excellent wisdom which is in us will support us
> (2 Bar. 48.20, 22-24).

The reply to Baruch's prayer centers first upon the theme of judgment. God tells Baruch that nothing will be destroyed unless it deserves to be destroyed: 'There is nothing that will be destroyed unless it acted wickedly, if it had been able to do something without remembering my goodness and longsuffering'.[56] Baruch is further told that he personally will be preserved. 'For this reason surely you will be taken up, as I said to you before'.[57] A description of the great wickedness coming at the end of times follows. This prompts Baruch to lament over those who have followed the sin of Adam and Eve and therefore, will experience the great judgment.

> O Adam, what did you do to all who were born after you? And what will be said of Eve who obeyed the serpent, so that this whole multitude is going to corruption? And countless are those whom the fire devours (2 Bar. 48.42-43).

Baruch lays the guilt at the feet of Adam and Eve for all the wickedness which has been described.[58] Notice that God is not accused of wrongdoing for bringing judgment upon humanity, but the blame is placed squarely upon humanity's shoulders, further showing the change in Baruch. This is followed by Baruch's confession of the justness of the judgment coming upon humanity, because it had transgressed the law (2 Bar. 48.45-47). Here individual responsibility for the judgment is laid at the feet of people themselves, because they have transgressed the law. The mention of transgression of the law suggests that the judgment referred to here is judgment upon the Jewish nation. Baruch's espousal of human responsibility for the judgment shows how he has come full circle and accepted the premise with which the book started.

Baruch changes the course of the discussion and inquires about the future of the righteous, especially the form of the resurrection bodies (ch. 49). There follows a description of the resurrection bodies, both of the wicked and the righteous: as the bodies of the righteous will be made glorious, so the bodies of the wicked will be made hideous. Further, the glories of paradise promised to the righteous are contrasted with the anguishes which the wicked will suffer. Here as nearly everywhere else, the glories of the righteous are described only in contrast to the miseries of the wicked. This constitutes a subtle apology. The glorious future is described to draw attention away from the present suffering. The future glories of the righteous are only shown to be really glorious when it is seen that the wicked will suffer a corresponding agony. The future fate of the wicked is contrasted with the future blessing of the righteous to show that retribution will occur, and the wicked as well as the righteous will receive their just due.

Baruch's reply contrasts the present sufferings with the much greater sufferings which will happen at the end. 'The lamentations should be kept for the beginning of that coming torment; let the tears be laid down for the coming of that destruction which will then come'.[59] The righteous are thus encouraged to rejoice in the present sufferings, since these sufferings will not compare with those to come, and to look to the glorious future. The present sufferings are thereby dismissed on two accounts: they would not compare to the coming sufferings and would be forgotten in the glorious future.

Baruch then goes to the people and explains how what has come upon them is due to their sins and the wickedness of the nation. He exhorts them to follow God's law so that the same will not happen again. He emphasizes their responsibility, however, for whatever happens. God has been justified at human expense.

God's Judgment upon the Nations

The second concern running through 2 Baruch is the demand for judgment upon the nations. In the previous pages Baruch's concern for justice for the Jewish nation was traced. In the following pages the other major strand, his demand for judgment upon the nations, will be traced.

Section I. The first section introduces the disaster which gave rise to Baruch's crisis of faith. The announcement of the destruction of Jerusalem causes Baruch to question his beliefs both about the destiny of the Jewish nation and the destiny of the other nations, and, as a result, his beliefs about God himself. Baruch initially questions the justness of the destruction of Jerusalem since Israel is God's chosen nation. His second reaction is to demand judgment upon those nations more wicked than the Jewish nation.

When Baruch's questions about Israel fail to cause God to turn back the destruction, Baruch complains that the other nations who hate God will come and pollute the sanctuary.

> Your haters will come to this place and pollute your sanctuary,
> and carry off your heritage into captivity,
> and rule over them whom you love.
> And then they will go away again to the land of their idols,

> and boast before them.
> And what have you done to your great name? (2 Bar. 5.1)

Once again Baruch turns attention away from the sin of the people. His argument contains an implied contrast between the great wickedness of the nation which will destroy Jerusalem, and the comparatively less serious sins of the Jewish people. It turns attention away from the sin of the Jewish nation, hoping to avert the judgment coming upon Jerusalem. This type of argument can be called an anthropodicy,[60] since Baruch attempts to justify the actions of the people, rather than the actions of God. God's answer, however, does not turn from his condemnation of the sins of the Jewish people. God answers first by telling Baruch that the enemies will also be judged. As a more direct answer to Baruch's complaint, he assures Baruch that the enemies will have no reason to boast over the Jews, since they will not conquer Jerusalem.

Section II. The vision in section II graphically illustrates the promise God has just made to Baruch. After the angels take the holy vessels out of the temple in Jerusalem, they breach the walls and invite the enemy in. Thus God is justified in bringing judgment upon the Jews through the actions of the enemies, because God, not the enemies, is responsible for the destruction of Jerusalem. Making God responsible for the overthrow of Jerusalem undermines Baruch's earlier complaint. Baruch can proclaim injustice when those more wicked than the Jews overthrow the Jews, but it is harder when God overthrows them.

Section III. This section consists mainly of a lament given in response to the coming destruction of Jerusalem. In the first half of the lament, Baruch grieves over the catastrophe. In the second half, he directs his anger against Babylon.

> Now this I, Baruch, say to you, O Babylon: If you had lived in happiness and Zion it its glory, it would have been a great sorrow to us that you had been equal to Zion. But now, behold, the grief is infinite and the lamentation is immeasurable, because, behold, you are happy and Zion has been destroyed (2 Bar. 11.1-2).

In contrast to the first half of the lament, in the second half Baruch believes that retribution will come upon Babylon.

> The afternoon will not always burn nor will the rays of the sun always give light. Do not think and do not expect that you will

> always have happiness and joy, and do not raise yourself too much and do not oppress. For surely wrath will arise against you in its own time, because long-suffering is now held back, as it were, by reins (2 Bar. 12.2-4).

This expression of the hope that the Babylonians will receive retribution for their sins sometime in the future represents the first movement on the part of Baruch toward a resolution of his problems. It reflects a portion of the provisional answer given to him by God in section I (2 Bar. 5.1). Section IV begins with a continuation of this theme.

Section IV. In the first part of this section Baruch is instructed that he and those like him will be preserved until the end of time so that they can then tell the nations why the evil is happening to them and why they are being punished. This punishment will be retribution in the strict sense, since it will be due to their sins and clearly caused by God.[61]

> This means that if these happy cities will ever say, 'Why has the mighty God brought upon us this retribution?', you and those who are like you, those who have seen this evil and retribution coming over you and your nation in their own time, may say to them that the nations will be thoroughly punished. And this they may expect. And when they say in that time, 'When?', you will say to them:
>
> You who have drunk the clarified wine,
> you now drink its dregs,
> for the judgment of the Most High is impartial.
> Therefore, he did not spare his own sons first,
> but he afflicted them as his enemies because they sinned.
> Therefore, they were once punished,
> that they might be forgiven.
> But now, you nations and tribes, you are guilty,
> because you have trodden the earth all this time,
> and because you have used creation unrighteously.
> For I have always benefited you,
> and you have always denied the beneficence (2 Bar. 13.4-12).

The function of these verses, however, is not to justify God's punishment of the nations, but to justify God's punishment of the Jewish nation. In this passage a contrast is drawn between the promised punishment of the nations, strict retribution, and the punishment of the Jewish nation, which has a redemptive character. This contrasts how God deals differently with the Jewish nation than with the other nations. The Jewish nation is punished so that they can be forgiven. The promise of the future punishment of the other nations without forgiveness, makes God's punishment of the Jewish nation seem gracious in comparison. Baruch's initial charge of unfairness (5.1) is answered, because even though the righteous must suffer for the sins of the wicked, the suffering has a redemptive character.[62]

Section V. Baruch's prayer at the beginning of this section reflects his changed attitude: he no longer accuses God of unfairness but instead confesses his confidence in the afterlife. Baruch then learns that the end of time will be followed by a great judgment where all the sins of the wicked will be revealed as well as all the righteousness of the righteous (24.1-2). At that time God's long-suffering toward both the wicked and the righteous will be revealed. The concept of God's long-suffering and the idea of a final judgment both point to a time in the future when retribution will occur. God's long-suffering toward his people results in their forgiveness; toward the nations it results in their judgment.[63] The idea of a final judgment and the associated idea of the long-suffering of God serve a powerful function as theodicy. However, they represent almost a negative concept of theodicy. The emphasis was upon the judgment which will fall upon the wicked and the suffering this entails rather than upon the reward of the righteous. The righteous receive satisfaction and the justness of God was vindicated by the suffering of the wicked. Baruch's question which immediately follows the announcement of the judgment reveals this concern for judgment. 'I also know what has befallen me; but that which will happen to our enemies, I do not know, or when you will command your works'.[64] Baruch knows the suffering which he has experienced and has a good idea that he will experience more; he now wants to know when the wicked will also suffer and what this will entail. Baruch's concern for justice entails not only fair treatment for the righteous but also punishment for the wicked.

The answer to Baruch's request for knowledge about what will happen to the enemies and when it will happen confirms the function performed by the judgment of the wicked in the theodicy. The great sufferings experienced by the wicked at the end of times is described as a time of great tribulation, when men will give up hope (25.1-4). When Baruch asked how long the tribulation will last, he is told it has twelve parts; these parts are indications not of time, but of the increase of wickedness and suffering.

> In the first part: the beginning of commotions. In the second part: the slaughtering of the great. In the third part: the fall of many into death. . . . In the twelfth part: disorder and a mixture of all that has been before (2 Bar. 27.2-13).

Baruch was then told that its measure would be 'two parts: weeks of seven weeks'. After this the Messiah would come and usher in the glorious Messianic reign, which though a great blessing to the righteous, would only add to the torment of the wicked. 'But the souls of the wicked will the more waste away when they shall see all these things. For they know that their torment has come and that their perditions have arrived'.[65] Even the description of the blessing of the righteous points to the suffering of the wicked.

Section VI. The section begins with a lament by Baruch over the destruction of Jerusalem. In response to the lament, he receives a vision. The vision and the initial interpretation (chs. 36–40) offer a historical overview of the last days, especially emphasizing the fate of Zion's enemies. It describes the rise and fall of four kingdoms, with the last kingdom falling at the hand of God's Messiah who will rule until the world of corruption ends. This vision of history's end, coming after Baruch's lament, serves to give him hope that even though Jerusalem is destroyed, the destroyer nation will also be destroyed. 'Behold, the days will come when this kingdom that destroyed Zion once will be destroyed and it will be subjected to that which will come after it'.[66] Once again this passage functions as a negative theodicy; the punishment of the wicked justifies God and comforts the righteous.

Section VII. After an initial prayer and dialogue, Baruch receives a vision in which he sees a series of thirteen alternating bright and black waters. He prays for the interpretation of the vision. This prayer not only reflects the change in Baruch, but also the purpose of the visions of the eschaton. He praises God and calls him:

> the one who reveals to those who fear that which is prepared for them so that you may comfort them. You show your mighty works to those who do not know. You pull down the enclosure for those who have no experience and enlighten the darknesses, and reveal

> the secrets to those who are spotless, to those who subjected themselves to you and your Law in faith (2 Bar. 54.4-5).

The purpose of the visions is to comfort the righteous: Baruch appears comforted. In direct contrast to his earlier reaction (3.2; 10.6), he now praises the day of his birth. 'Blessed is my mother among those who bear, and praised among women is she who bore me'.[67] God's judgment is no longer questioned nor his justness in administering it. 'And those who do not love your Law are justly perishing. And the torment of judgment will fall upon those who have not subjected themselves to your power'.[68] The individual's responsibility for judgment or glory is emphasized.

> For, although Adam sinned first and brought death upon all who were not in his own time, yet each of them who has been born from him has prepared for himself the coming torment. And further, each of them has chosen for himself the coming glory. For truly, the one who believes will receive reward.
> Adam is, therefore, not the cause, except only for himself, but each of us has become our own Adam (2 Bar. 54.15-16, 19).

After these affirmations, Baruch asks for the interpretation of the vision, sure that it will reveal that retribution will occur; the wicked will receive in accordance with their wickedness and the righteous in accordance with their faith.

> For at the end of the world, a retribution will be demanded with regard to those who have done wickedly in accordance with their wickedness, and you will glorify the faithful ones in accordance with their faith (2 Bar. 54.21).

Baruch now understands the real Jewish nation as the righteous who follow God's law. 'For those who are among your own, you rule; and those who sin, you blot out among your own'.[69] All that remains for Baruch is for the course of history to be explained to him, especially as regarding the retribution at the end.

The interpretation of the vision of waters is a historical overview beginning from creation and the time of Adam to the Messianic reign. The reason for the vision, its value, and its interpretation are given by Baruch in his prayer in response to the interpretation. The vision gives those who know God and follow his laws the reason for their existence.

> But we who exist, when we know why we have come,
> and then subject ourselves to him who brought us out of Egypt,
> we will come again and remember those things which have passed away,
> and rejoice with regard to the things which have been (2 Bar. 75.7).

The historical vision in section VII functions in the theodicy to offer hope that history is indeed moving toward the time when retribution will occur. It offers Baruch an answer to both of his initial concerns: the righteous will receive the good they deserve and the wicked will receive the punishment they deserve.

D. *Eschatology*

As could be expected after the analysis of the literary structure and the theodicy argument, the eschatological sections are mainly in the last half of the book. The various passages speaking of eschatological matters do not always seem to have the same view of what will happen at the end of times. Second Baruch, however, does not intend to present a detailed eschatological view; rather the eschatology is presented with an apologetic intent. The eschatological passages serve the theodicy.

Like the theodicy, the eschatology has two main threads: one concerns the fate of the righteous and the other fate of the wicked. The two threads are so intertwined, however, that they will be analyzed together. The eschatology of the righteous reflects the same tension discovered in the analysis of the theodicy, namely, the individual righteous person versus the Jewish nation.[70] The eschatology of the nation is found mainly in the Messianic kingdom, which in 2 Baruch is of a temporary nature. The eschatology of the individual, though mainly focusing on resurrection, also takes over many of the ideas of the Messianic kingdom where the individual righteous assume the place of the nation as God's chosen. The eschatology of the evil nations and the eschatology of the individual wicked are not distinguished, and are described mainly in terms of the final judgment.

Sections I to III

The first half of 2 Baruch, occupied mainly with the description of Jerusalem's destruction and Baruch's initial reaction, has little eschatological content of either an individual or national nature. Throughout sections I through III, Baruch is repeatedly assured that the coming destruction is only 'for a time' (Syriac, *'d zbn'*, *lzbn'* or *bzbn'*).

> Behold, therefore, I shall bring evil upon this city and its inhabitants. And it will be taken away from before my presence for a time.
>
> This city will be delivered up for a time,
> And the people will be chastened for a time,
> And the world will not be forgotten.
>
> For the time has arrived when Jerusalem will also be
> delivered up for a time,
> until the moment that it will be said to be restored forever (2 Bar. 1.4; 4.1; 6.9).

These vague references give little information other than that the destruction is only temporary. Section I vaguely refers to a heavenly Jerusalem.

> It is not this building that is in your midst now; it is that which will be revealed, with me, that was already prepared from the moment that I decided to create Paradise (2 Bar. 4.3).

The mention of the heavenly Jerusalem assures Baruch that the destruction does not have the finality which he assumed, and thereby emphasizes the temporary nature of the destruction. The lack of references to the heavenly Jerusalem in the latter eschatological passages confirms this understanding.[71]

The description of the fate of Babylon (12.3-5) gives the most detailed eschatolgical view of any passage in sections I through III. Babylon is warned that her prosperity will not last forever, but (divine) wrath, then held back, will fall upon her.

> The afternoon will not always burn nor will the rays of the sun always give light. Do not think and do not expect that you will always have happiness and joy, and do not raise yourself too much and do not oppress. For surely wrath will arise against you in its own time, because long-suffering is now held back, as it were, by reins (2 Bar. 12.2-5).

These verses plainly function in the theodicy to emphasize that the present prosperity of the wicked will not last and that retribution will come upon them in eschaton.

The vague references to eschatological concepts in sections I through III are considerably expanded throughout the rest of the book, occupying the center of attention.

Section IV

This section mentions for the first time the future of the righteous. The righteous spoken of in this passage are the individual righteous Jews as shown by the analysis of the theodicy (see Section C IV above). The future inbreak of God is described as the 'end of times' (13.3) and the time when God will 'visit' the world (20.2). For the righteous as well as the wicked, the end of time will be a time of tribulation, for the righteous will experience the same evil as the wicked. 'Woe to those of us who have also now been treated shamefully and who await evils at that time'.[72] The righteous, however, look to the world promised to them by God in which they will be rewarded according to their good works (14.12-13). This future world for the righteous is described as a 'crown with great glory' (15.8) and as being immeasurable (16.1). The wicked can expect only judgment at the end (13.6).

The end of time is rapidly approaching and in fact the judgment upon Zion has hastened its coming. 'Therefore, I now took away Zion to visit the world in its own time more speedily'.[73] A periodic conception of history serves as the background of this passage and is referred to later on. In 14.1 Baruch said that God has shown him the 'course of the times'.[74]

Section V

The section begins with a prayer of Baruch containing many hints but few details about the eschaton. We find that God is the only one who knows when the end will come (21.8b), and only he knows the end of the wicked and the fulfillment of the righteous (21.12). The importance of this eschatology to the theodicy becomes clearer when Baruch argues there must be another life because this life is so bitter.

> You know where you have preserved the end of those who have sinned or the fulfillment of those who have proved themselves to be righteous. For if only this life exists which everyone possesses here, nothing could be more bitter than this.... For if an end of all things had not been prepared, their beginning would have been senseless (2 Bar. 21.12-13, 17).

God assures Baruch that the end will come and the world will not be finished until then.

> Baruch, Baruch, why are you disturbed? Who starts a journey and does not complete it?... Or he who plants a vineyard—does the planter expect to receive fruit from it, unless it grows until its appointed time? (2 Bar. 22.2-3, 6).

In the course of attempting to convince Baruch of the certainty of the end, God says that resurrection is the destiny of the righteous.

> When Adam sinned and death was decreed against those who were to be born, the multitude of those who would be born was numbered. And for that number a place was prepared where the living ones might live and where the dead might be preserved. No creature will live again unless the number that has been appointed is completed. For my spirit creates the living, and the realm of death receives the dead (2 Bar. 23.4-5).

This passage gives little detail about the resurrection,[75] since the resurrection is mentioned only to emphasize the certainty of the end. An intermediate state, 'where the living ones might live and where the dead might be preserved', also seems implied. Other than this vague reference to the resurrection, the only information given is that until the end, the dead reside in the realm of the dead. No distinction is made between different intermediate states or different ultimate fates of the righteous and the wicked. The different ultimate fates of the righteous and the wicked are distinguished in the next chapter, where the judgment is describes in traditional terms.

> For behold, the days are coming, and the books will be opened in which are written the sins of all those who have sinned, and moreover, also the treasuries in which are brought together the righteousness of all those who have proven themselves to be righteous. And it will happen at that time that you shall see, and many with you, the long-suffering of the Most High, which lasts from generation to generation, who has been long-suffering toward all who are born, both those who sinned and those who proved themselves to be righteous (2 Bar. 24.1-2).

Once again the description, lacking detail about the eschaton since it is more concerned to serve the theodicy, emphasizes that God has been merciful with everyone, both righteous and sinner.

In reply to Baruch's questions about the time and duration of the tribulation, he learns that the final tribulation, having twelve parts further describing the tribulation suffering (ch. 27), will last a week of seven weeks (28.2). All the world will experience the tribulation, but God will protect those found in the holy land (29.1-2).

At the end of the tribulation the Messiah will be revealed (29.3) to usher in a period of prosperity. Earth's inhabitants will be sustained by God during that period. The time is called the consummation of times (29.8) and is described as a period of limited duration during which the Messiah will reign and after which the Messiah will return to heaven with glory (30.1).[76] 'All who sleep in hope of him' will be resurrected after Messiah's return to glory (30.1b). Until that time the souls of the righteous will be kept in treasuries (30.2). The souls of the wicked will also survive death, but they will waste away all the more when they see the resurrection of the righteous (30.4), 'for they know that their torment has come and that their perditions have arrived'.[77]

After Baruch learns these details about 'the end of times', he goes to reassure the people (chs. 31–32). In this speech he emphasizes that the present earthly temple is only temporary and will soon be rebuilt in glory. The end time he describes as a time when God will shake the entire creation and send greater trials than all the evils experienced now. With this passage (chs. 31–32) the function of the description of the tribulation evils becomes clear. The greater evil of the time of tribulation overshadows the present evil and mitigates it by comparison. 'We should not, therefore, be so sad regarding the evil which has come now, but much more (distressed) regarding that which is in the future'.[78]

Section VI

Baruch goes once again to the temple to weep and mourn the destruction of Jerusalem. In response he receives a vision (chs. 35–37) which tells of four kingdoms and their eventual downfall, culminating in the time of the Messiah who at the beginning of his rule, will convict and punish the last ruler. This vision obviously intends to show the transitory nature of these evil nations and the imminence of the end times characterized by the Messianic period. This intent was plainly in the admonition to Baruch to remember and understand what has been revealed to him, for it is his consolation.

> You, however, Baruch, strengthen your heart with a view to that which has been said to you, and understand that which has been revealed to you because you have many consolations which will last forever (2 Bar. 43.1).

Baruch's speech to the people further emphasizes this intent (ch. 44). He assures them that better times are coming and that the present evils will not be remembered. The present time and its unhappiness are nothing and will be forgotten; the future, however, will be very great.

Section VII

This section begins with Baruch's prayer for God's mercy upon the people. God replies to this request by referring to his judgment and describing the tribulations of the end time. The tribulation will be a time of judgment, thus a time of affliction, enormous vehemence, and the heat of indignation. It will be a time of false peace, a time when wisdom will not be found, a time of miracles and wonders, and a time when good will change to evil. Finally, at the end, what is happening will become evident to those on earth; this will only increase their torment.

Baruch then asks about the form of the righteous after the resurrection (ch. 49). The description which follows is of a two-stage resurrection (chs. 50–51). First the dead will be raised in their original bodies. After they recognize one another, the judgment will occur. Within the context of 2 Baruch and the emphasis upon the judgment in this passage, the reason for the first stage of the resurrection is so that the wicked might recognize the righteous and so be tormented all the more by their later transformation.[79] After the first stage of the resurrection, the bodies of the resurrected will be transformed; the evil will become more evil in shape and the righteous more glorious. The torment of the wicked will thus increase. The righteous, however, will perceive the invisible world and inhabit it (51.8-10); paradise will be spread out before them. Time will no longer hold sway over them (51.9). The righteousness of the righteous will exceed that of the angels. Within 2 Baruch, this description of the resurrection life overshadows the present sufferings of the righteous,[80] functioning in the theodicy as partial justification for the present suffering of the righteous.[81]

After the dialogue about the resurrection, Baruch sees a vision of a series of twelve black and bright waters followed by one final pair of black and bright waters (ch. 53). The vision is interpreted (chs. 54–74) as a historical overview, beginning with the time of the sin of Adam and culminating in the Messianic kingdom. The final waters were the tribulation and the Messianic reign. The tribulation will be a time of evil and confusion (see chs. 70–71). People will hate one another and provoke one another to fight. The tribulation will culminate in a great war (70.7-10) instigated by God himself. At the end of the war the Messiah will appear and establish control over all, both victor and loser. Those in the holy land, however, will be protected from the war. When the Messiah comes he will judge all the nations, sparing some and destroying others (ch. 72). This will usher in the period of the Messianic bliss. 'That time is the end of that which is corruptible and the beginning of that which is incorruptible.'[82]

The timetable in this passage agrees fairly well with the other passages mentioning the final tribulation and the following Messianic reign. The one addition in this passage is the mention of the final war which ushers in the Messianic era. The final war functions in the theodicy as one more reason for hope that the wicked will receive the punishment they deserve and the righteous the victory over the wicked they deserve.

If 2 Baruch had a consistent eschatological timetable, the timetable would be something like the following. The end of time would begin with the tribulation, marked by an increase of wickedness and war. At the end of the tribulation, the Messiah would come to fight, subdue, and render judgment upon all the nations. This would usher in the period of Messianic bliss. The Messiah's return to glory would mark the end of the Messianic reign and time itself. It would immediately precede the resurrection and the final judgment.

E. *The Function of Eschatology*

Eschatological ideas play a major role in 2 Baruch. The presentation of these ideas does not intend, however, to supply esoteric data about the eschaton, but rather to offer help to the person struggling with the problem of evil. In this way it contributes to the overall purpose of the book. Generally, the exposition of eschatological ideas function in the theodicy to offer proof that retribution will occur; the wicked will be punished for their wickedness and the righteous will be rewarded for their righteousness. The eschatological ideas can be divided into three basic categories, each answering a specific problem. For the righteous individual, the eschaton means resurrection to eternal life, entry into paradise, and reward. The Jewish nation can look forward to the period of Messianic rule when Israel's enemies will be conquered and subdued and Jerusalem will be restored. The wicked nations will be conquered by the Messiah when he returns and all the wicked will be delivered up at the final judgment.

Four passages discuss the resurrection: 23.4-5; 30.1-5; 42.7; 50.1–52.7. Resurrection is first mentioned only in passing (23.4-5) to help reassure Baruch that time will end. This mention of the resurrection is sketchy and is only intended to support the argument about the certainty of the end. The other three passages (30.1-5; 42.7; 50.1–52.7) have a similar function. The resurrection is pictured as the time when the injustices of this world will be corrected. This primarily means the time when the wicked will be punished for their wickedness; both 30.1-5 and 42.7 mention the resurrection only in connection with judgment. Chapters 50 to 52 give a rather elaborate description of the resurrection/exaltation of the righteous; however, this description also comes in the midst of a description of judgment. For the individual, resurrection is the eschatological description of future retribution.

God initially answers Baruch's concern about the downfall of Jerusalem by emphasizing that the destruction is only 'for a time', after which Jerusalem will be restored (chs. 1–4). Baruch is not satisfied with this initial answer, however, since it does not right the injustice of the wicked nations going unpunished. Baruch is further assured that the wicked nations will be punished. As the theme of judgment upon the wicked nations is developed, the description of the judgment becomes more detailed. Judgment upon the nations is associated with the related ideas of the tribulation (26.1–28.7; 48.30-41; 70.1–71.2) and the Messiah (29.1-30.5; 48.40-41; 72.1–74.4). When the Messiah comes, he will conquer and punish all the nations and bring a period of Messianic bliss, when he will rule from Jerusalem. Thus the enemies will be destroyed and the nation restored. The return of the Messiah is for the Jewish nation the time when retribution will occur.

The topic of the punishment of the wicked occupies most of the eschatological material, including both the punishment of the wicked nations by the Messiah and the final judgment after the resurrection. The concern for judgment is present in all the eschatological passages, if not the central topic. The passages mentioning the reward of the righteous, however, contrast the reward of the righteous with judgment upon the wicked (note 50.1–51.16; 73.1–74.4).

Eschatology in 2 Baruch serves theodicy by showing that retribution will happen in the future.

Chapter 5

ESCHATOLOGY AS THEODICY IN 2 BARUCH AND 4 EZRA

Second Baruch and Fourth Ezra present an interesting study in different approaches to the same problem. Both works address the problem which the destruction of Jerusalem in 70 CE caused the Jewish people and arrive at basically the same answer. Neither work saw any hope of a reconciliation of their problems in the present, but instead looked to the future when the present world order would be overthrown and retribution would occur. The ways in which they arrived at this position, however, were very different.

A. *Comparison and Contrast of 2 Baruch and 4 Ezra*

A literary relationship has often been suggested between 2 Baruch and 4 Ezra. Not only do they both deal with the same issue in much the same manner, they also express the same ideas in much the same language.[1] This study has confirmed that, though they have many similarities, they also have many differences. The following section will look at these similarities and differences in the structure of both books, the different theodicies they present, the different issues their theodicies address, and the different ways they both use eschatology in their theodicies.

Structure

The literary structure of 2 Baruch and 4 Ezra is similar only on a broad scale. Both works have a seven-section structure and use dialogues extensively. But there the structural parallels end.[2] The grouping and uses of the sections are different in each book. The examination of the differences can further illumine each book's purpose.

The seven sections of 2 Baruch divide easily into two groups which split the book and the theodicy in halves. The sections within each half are similar in structure. In the first half, section I through IV, God initiates the contacts and the major topic of discussion is God's justice. In the second half, sections V through VII, Baruch initiates the contacts and the major topic of discussion is eschatology and how eschatological ideas answer the questions raised in the first half.

The seven sections in 4 Ezra have a very different grouping. The first two sections are parallel in structure and content and function to present the problem which the book addresses. The second two sections are also parallel in structure and content and serve to present the solution to the problem presented in the first two sections. In contrast 2 Baruch, where God initiates the contacts and sets the agenda for discussion in the first four sections, in 4 Ezra, Ezra initiates the contacts and sets the agenda for the discussion. The third pair of sections, sections V and VI, once again has a parallel structure and functions to portray graphically, through visions, the solution reached in the previous two sections. In these two sections God initiates the contacts, reversing the earlier pattern. The last section adds little to the argument and is considered an epilogue.

The differences reflect the different arguments and the different tone of each book. For example, in 2 Baruch, God was the first initiator of contact and set the parameters for the following discussion (2 Bar. 1.1), whereas in 4 Ezra, Ezra was the first to initiate contact and set the parameters of the discussion. This subtle difference reflects the different tone of each work.[3] Second Baruch presents the eschatological answers to the problem of evil in a rather straightforward manner, with little objection on the part of Baruch. God controls the discussion throughout and leads Baruch to the resolution of his problems. 4 Ezra is characterized by the objections and complaints of Ezra regarding the problem of evil. Ezra begins the discussion and seems in control throughout; only with difficulty are his problems solved and even then a certain uneasiness about the solution remains. It is almost as if 2 Baruch presents the theodicy from God's side and 4 Ezra from man's side, or to use Berger's categories (see Chapter 1), 2 Baruch mainly addresses the problem of theodicy (the justice of God), whereas 4 Ezra often confronts the problem of anthropodicy (the problem of sin).[4] The different initiator or contact in each book reflects the different intent of each book. The divergent structures of 2 Baruch and 4 Ezra only hint at the broad differences in the theodicies of each book.[5]

Theodicy

The theodicy in 2 Baruch works on three levels. The problem of retribution for the righteous individual is answered with the promise of resurrection to eternal life and entry into paradise. The Jewish nation can look forward to a period of messianic rule when Israel's enemies will be conquered and Jerusalem will be restored. The justice of God is upheld because the wicked nations will be conquered by the Messiah and all the wicked will be delivered up at the final judgment.

In 4 Ezra, retribution, as found in the doctrine of sin, clashes with the doctrine of future retribution. The present evils are ample evidence of the sinfulness of the people. In light of this sinfulness, what good are promises of retribution in the future, since righteousness is the prerequisite of inheriting the promises? The answer to this problem is found in the mercy of God.

An interesting contrast between 2 Baruch and 4 Ezra is the place of the wicked in each of the arguments. In 2 Baruch one of Baruch's key demands is retribution upon the enemies. His demand for justice includes not only fair treatment of the righteous but also ample punishment for the wicked. In 4 Ezra, because of the universality of sin, the punishment of the wicked is lamented and Ezra pleads for mercy upon the wicked. Ezra does not demand that the wicked be punished as much as he pleads for mercy upon the righteous.[6]

The use of eschatology differs in 2 Baruch and 4 Ezra. In 2 Baruch, eschatology is much more prominent and more concern is given to the specific ways in which eschatological matters answer specific theodicy questions. For example, resurrection is the main answer for the individual and the messianic reign for the nation. In 4 Ezra, the validity of the eschatological answer is questioned. Only after the problem of sin and the eschatological promise is resolved does the author of 4 Ezra turn to eschatological matters in any detail.

The solutions to the problem of theodicy in both books are very different, but they were also much alike. When confronting the religious problems which the present evils presented, both books despair of finding the answer in the present world and look to the world beyond.

B. *Jewish Theodicy and 2 Baruch and 4 Ezra*

Second Baruch and Fourth Ezra have been designated in this study as narrative theodicies. As such they have drawn upon nearly all the previous types of Jewish theodicy surveyed in the first chapter in their attempts to make sense of the problem of evil. For both, the central theodicy concept is future retribution. Neither work, however, simply accepts the doctrine of future retribution without argument. They both marshal other arguments in the service of their struggle with theodicy.

Both 2 Baruch and 4 Ezra are very much ruled by the doctrine of retribution, formulated as the doctrine of sin. The opening words of 2 Baruch illustrate this well.

> Have you seen all that this people are doing to me, the evil things which the two tribes which remained have done—more than the ten tribes which were carried away into captivity? For the former tribes were forced by their kings to sin, but these two have themselves forced and compelled their kings to sin. Behold, therefore, I shall bring evil upon this city and its inhabitants (2 Bar. 1.1-4a; cf. 4 Ezra 3.1-11).

For both works, especially 2 Baruch, the fact that the fall of Jerusalem is attributable to the sins of the people goes without saying and is basically unquestioned. The way in which this fact is understood and the ramifications it has for theodicy differs in the two books.

Second Baruch marshals more differing arguments to buttress its theodicy than 4 Ezra. Not only are the righteous promised retribution in the future, but the present evils are said to have a disciplinary or redemptive character. The disciplinary nature of the present suffering was hinted at from the very start.

> And I shall scatter this people among the nations that they may do good to the nations. And my people will be chastened, and the time will come that they will look for that which can make their times prosperous (2 Bar. 1.4b-5).

The inadequacy of this answer is shown by its being virtually ignored in the rest of the book. The idea of the redemptive nature of suffering plays a larger role. Baruch is told that the chosen people are punished first so that they might be forgiven.

> Therefore, he did not spare his own sons first,
> but he afflicted them as his enemies because they sinned.
> Therefore, they were once punished,
> that they might be forgiven (2 Bar. 13.9-10).

The destruction of Jerusalem is even said to speed the advent of the end. 'Therefore, I now took away Zion to visit the world in its own time more speedily'.[7] The main answer in 2 Baruch, however, is that retribution will happen in the future. Different eschatological schemes are used to give answers to different problems, but no new answers are found in 2 Baruch.

Fourth Ezra presents the clash of the doctrine of retribution with the doctrine of future retribution. Unlike 2 Baruch, 4 Ezra does not explain the present suffering with the disciplinary, probationary, or redemptive arguments. The author of 4 Ezra realizes that if sin is used to explain present evil, then sin will also negate the future hope. Strict retribution results in the damnation of all.

> For what does it profit us that we shall be preserved alive but cruelly tormented? For all who have been born are involved in iniquities, and are full of sins and burdened with transgressions. And if we were not to come into judgment after death, perhaps it would have been better for us (4 Ezra 7.67-69).

The rational and irrational ends of the theodicy continuum have thus been bent around to meet one another and the inadquacy of any theodicy which relies on retribution has been shown.[8] The author of 4 Ezra found his theodicy in the mercy of God and retained retribution only in its most irrational form—future retribution. The mercy of God was something which only could be experienced and not proven, thus 4 Ezra did not try to demonstrate by rational means the solution which the theodicy offered. The answer was found, in the final analysis, in a religious experience, not much different from the answer found by Job. 4 Ezra did not offer any new answers to the theodicy question, it sought a melding of the answers of religious experience and future retribution, and further demonstrated the inadequacy of the rational answer.

NOTES

Notes to Chapter 1

1. Some recent efforts to understand the problem of evil include: John Hick, *Evil and the God of Love* (2nd edn, London: Macmillan, 1977); Austin Farrer, *Love Almighty and Ills Unlimited* (Garden City, N.Y.: Doubleday, 1961); Francois Petit, *The Problem of Evil* (trans. Christopher Williams; New York: Hawthorn, 1959); Nelson Pike, ed., *God and Evil* (Englewood Cliffs, N.J.: Prentice-Hall, 1965).

2. Jeremiah 12.1b, RSV.

3. David Hume, *Dialogues Concerning Natural Religion*, ed. Henry D. Aiken (New York: Hafner, 1948), p. 66.

4. Leibniz's theory was brilliantly satirized by Voltaire in *Candide*.

5. Walther Eichrodt, 'Faith in Providence and Theodicy in the Old Testament', in James L. Crenshaw, ed., *Theodicy in the Old Testament* (Issues in Religion and Theology, 4; Philadelphia: Fortress, 1983), p. 27.

6. Peter L. Berger, *The Sacred Canopy: Elements of a Sociological Theory of Religion* (Garden City, N.Y.: Doubleday, 1967), pp. 54-55.

7. Berger (p. 78) called this effort to justify man anthropodicy.

8. Ibid., pp. 54-80.

9. Two recent Jewish theodicies illustrate this. On the rational end of the continuum Harold S. Kushner, *When Bad Things Happen to Good People* (New York: Schocken Books, 1981) decided that God must be limited in power, else he would have stopped evil. Moving away from rationality, Robert Gordis, 'A Cruel God or None—Is There No Choice?' *Judaism* 21 (1972), pp. 277-84, despairing of a resolution of evil in this life, opted for meaning in the Messianic era.

10. Since Klaus Koch's article 'Gibt es ein Vergeltungsdogma im Alten Testament?', *ZTK* 52 (1955), pp. 1-42, many have followed Koch and denied a doctrine of retribution exists in the Old Testament. See the discussion below for further details and arguments.

11. Ibid. An English translation of the major portion of the article can be found in *Theodicy in the Old Testament*, 'Is There a Doctrine of Retribution in the Old Testament?', pp. 57-87.

12. For the reaction to Koch, see the summary of the discussion and the literature cited in John G. Gammie, 'The Theology of Retribution in the Book of Deuteronomy', *CBQ* 32 (1970), pp. 1-5.

13. William McKane, *Proverbs*: *A New Approach* (The Old Testament Library; Philadelphia: Westminster, 1970), p. 11. His assumption about the chronological development from 'old wisdom' to Yahwistic wisdom is not accepted by this writer.

14. McKane classified the strictly wisdom proverbs as Class A and the ones expressing Yahwistic piety as Class C.

15. Ibid., p. 420. He apparently had the narrower concept of theodicy in mind—a strictly rational system.

16. For example, Koch's analysis of Hosea is correct; see *Theodicy in the Old Testament*, pp. 64-69. The view of recompense in Hosea is one in which Yahweh has no direct hand. It is used, however, to absolve Yahweh of complicity in the evil which is happening to Israel and therefore a type of theodicy.

17. That it is basic was the judgment of Walther Eichrodt, *Theology of the Old Testament* (trans. J.A. Baker; The Old Testament Library; Philadelphia: Westminster, 1961), II, p. 484.

18. For further examples see those listed as Class C in McKane, *Proverbs*, pp. 415, 428, 441, 452, 463, 476, 487, 501, 513, 523, 536, 579, 620, 632.

19. See J. Kenneth Kuntz, 'The Retribution Motif in *Psalmic Wisdom*', *ZAW* 89 (1977), pp. 223-33, who classified Pss. 1; 25.12-14; 32; 40.5-6; 128 in this same category.

20. James L. Crenshaw ('Introduction: the Shift from Theodicy to Anthropodicy', *Theodicy in the Old Testament*, pp. 1-16), following Berger (*The Sacred Canopy*, p. 74), traced a chronological development from an emphasis on justification of God to a justification of man. Thus the development would be in the opposite direction from that asserted by McKane; see note 12. My conclusion is that the development is parallel not chronological.

21. E. Würthwein, 'The Old Testament Belief in Recompense', *Theological Dictionary of the New Testament*, ed. Gerhard Kittel (trans. and ed. Geoffrey W. Bromiley; Grand Rapids: Eerdmans, 1967), IV, p. 711. Compare also the comments of Eichrodt, 'Faith in Providence and Theodicy in the Old Testament', p. 27, on this prophetic conception.

22. See Alden L. Thompson, *Responsibility for Evil in the Theodicy of IV Ezra* (Society of Biblical Literature Dissertation Series, 29; Missoula, Mont.: Scholar's Press, 1977), ch. 1, especially p. 19, for a recent summary of the theories of the origin of evil.

23. Arthur S. Peake, *The Problem of Suffering in the Old Testament* (London: Epworth, 1904), pp. 65-72.

24. This idea is by no means confined to the prophetic literature. For examples from the Deuteronomic literature see Gammie, 'The theology of Retribution in the Book of Deuteronomy', pp. 6-10. For the Psalms see Kuntz, 'The Retribution Motif in Psalmic Wisdom', pp. 228–32. For the

apocalyptic literature see W. Sibley Towner, 'Retributional Theology in the Apocalyptic Setting', *USQR* 26 (1971), pp. 203-14. For Lamentations see Robert Davidson, *The Courage to Doubt*: *Exploring an Old Testament Theme* (London: SCM, 1983), pp. 155-60.

25. Eichrodt, *Theology of the Old Testament*, II, p. 488. He also listed further examples.

26. Cf. Crenshaw, *Theodicy in the Old Testament*, p. 7; Gerhard von Rad, *Das Geschichtsbild des chronistischen Werkes* (BWANT, 54; Stuttgart: Kohlhammer, 1930), pp. 10-14. The Deuteronomic history emphasizes collective retribution, whereas the Chronicler's history emphasizes individual retribution; see below.

27. Stanley Brice Frost, 'The Death of Josiah: A Conspiracy of Silence', *JBL* 87 (1968), pp. 367-82.

28. 2 Chron. 35.18.

29. 2 Chron. 33.9.

30. According to Hume's dichotomy, the goodness of God was sacrificed; see p. 1. the opening paragraph of this book.

31. Berger (*The Sacred Canopy*, p. 60) would classify such a theodicy, which explains the misfortune of an individual in terms of the collective, as the ultimate in irrationality. This judgment fails to take account of the level on which the theodicy works, the individual or the collective. The Deuteronomic history obviously works on the collective level.

32. See the previous discussion for details.

33. Gammie ('The Theology of Retribution in the Book of Deuteronomy', p. 12), pointed to Deut. 24.16 as early evidence of the breakdown of the collective theory of retribution.

34. Ezek. 18.2, RSV; see also Jer. 31.29-30.

35. Eichrodt (*Theology of the Old Testament*, II, pp. 433-86) gave a concise discussion of the issue, pointing to the irrationality of explaining an individual's misfortune by the collective's sin (p. 484). Berger also would see irrationality, but so do the people.

36. For Qoheleth, the theory of recompense had a definite religious dimension. When the theory broke down so also did the vitality of his faith. Qoheleth no longer had any good reason to have faith, he believed, simply because he saw no other alternatives. See Davidson, *The Courage to Doubt*, pp. 184-202. This, of course, contradicts Koch and his followers.

37. Gerhard von Rad, *Wisdom in Israel* (trans. J.D. Martin; New York: Abingdon, 1972), p. 107.

38. Koch, 'Is There a Doctrine of Retribution in the Old Testament?', *Theodicy in the Old Testament*, pp. 79-80; Hartmut Gese, 'The Crisis of Wisdom in Koheleth', *Theodicy in the Old Testament*, p. 143.

39. Eccl. 3.1, RSV.

40. Eccl. 3.22, RSV.

41. Jim Alvin Sanders, *Suffering as Divine Discipline in the Old Testament and Post-Biblical Judaism* (Colgate Rochester Divinity School Bulletin, 28; Rochester, N.Y.: Colgate Rochester Divinity School, 1955) gave the most complete listing of passages with this idea in them; see p. 44. Sanders, however, restricted himself to passages containing the word *yasar*, which does not exhaust the idea. See also O.S. Rankin, *Israel's Wisdom Literature: Its Bearing on Theology and the History of Religion* (Edinburgh: T. & T. Clark, 1936), pp. 19-22.

42. See Deut. 8.3, 5. Gammie, 'The Theology of Retribution in the Book of Deuteronomy', p. 11.

43. Eichrodt, 'Faith in Providence and Theodicy in the Old Testament', *Theodicy in the Old Testament*, p. 21.

44. This terminology comes from O.S. Rankin, *Israel's Wisdom Literature*, p. 19.

45. Ronald J. Williams, 'Theodicy in the Ancient Near East', *Canadian Journal of Theology* 2 (1956), p. 22.

46. Gammie, 'The Theology of Retribution in the Book of Deuteronomy', p. 10. The biblical citation is Deut. 8.2 (RSV).

47. See for example, Deut. 8.1-5, where the ideas of probationary and disciplinary suffering occur together, which is followed by a warning for the people not to begin thinking of themselves as righteous.

48. Berger, *The Sacred Canopy*, p. 58.

49. See Eichrodt, 'Faith in Providence and Theodicy in the Old Testament', *Theodicy in the Old Testament*, p. 33; Gerhard von Rad, 'The Confessions of Jeremiah', *Theodicy in the Old Testament*, pp. 88-99.

50. Jer. 15.15.

51. The warning by von Rad about over-interpretation of Jeremiah's sufferings as having inherent atoning power is prudent. See von Rad, 'The Confessions of Jeremiah', *Theodicy in the Old Testament*, pp. 98-99.

52. A recent Jewish version of the argument is Robert Gordis, 'A Cruel God or None—Is There No Choice?' On the Christian side, Immanuel Kant's arguments have had a continuing effect on Christian theology. Kant, arguing from the moral necessity of retribution, postulated both eternal life, in which retribution would occur, and the existence of God. See Immanuel Kant, *Critique of Practical Reason* (trans. L.W. Beck; Indianapolis: Bobbs-Merril, The Liberal Arts Press, 1956), II. 2, Sections 4 & 5.

53. Kuntz ('The Retribution Motif in Psalmic Wisdom', pp. 230-31) did not classify these psalms as having a future orientation; he reserved this classification for the other-worldly type.

54. See also Psalm 112, especially vv. 7-8.

55. Gerhard von Rad (*Wisdom in Israel*, p. 204), wisely pointed out that our knowledge of ideas about life after death in post-Exilic Judaism is inadequate to rule out such an interpretation *a priori*.

56. See Kuntz, 'The Retribution Motif in Psalmic Wisdom', p. 231; he also found this motif in Ps. 73.23-26 (EVV, vv. 24-27).

57. Compare also e.g. Mal. 2.17–3.5; 4.1-3; Isa. 42.14-17; 44.24–45.13; 47.1-15; Jer. 31.27-34.

58. Donald E. Gowan, *The Triumph of Faith in Habakkuk* (Atlanta: John Knox, 1976).

59. Compare Otto Kaiser, *Isaiah 13–39: A Commentary* (The Old Testament Library; Philadelphia: Westminster, 1974), pp. 192-96, who understood these verses as bordering on, if not, apocalyptic; and Gerhard von Rad, *The Message of the Prophets* (trans. D.M.G. Stalker; New York: Harper & Row, 1962), pp. 89-94, who would deny any otherworldly eschatological emphasis in the Old Testament at all.

60. Compare the remarks of Hans Walter Wolff, *Joel and Amos: A Commentary on the Books of the Prophets Joel and Amos* (Hermeneia; trans. Waldemar Janzen, S. Dean McBride, Jr, & Charles A. Muenchow; ed. S. Dean McBride, Jr; Philadelphia: Fortress, 1977), p. 86, concerning Joel 4 (EVV, 3). 'The light of the promise casts its rays beyond the fulfillment that has taken place [The coming of Christ into history]. . . . the New Testament people of God together with the Old Testament people of God are waiting for a future event which will exceed the bounds of the old expectation'.

61. Besides the Isaiah Apocalypse, mentioned in the text and Joel 4 (EVV,3) mentioned in the preceding note, see also Zech. 10.3 and the commentaries on these passages.

62. The book of Jonah presents an unusual type of theodicy which does not fit easily into the present classification system. The problem for Jonah could be stated: 'Are God's compassionate actions just?' See Terence E. Fretheim, 'Jonah and Theodicy', *ZAW* 90 (1978), pp. 227-37. Jonah learned that, yes, the compassion of God is just. The sovereignty of God overruled the question of justice, working similarly to this type.

63. This assumes that the epilogue and prologue are not a part of the original book. The epilogue, along with the prologue, assumed that Job's suffering was a result of a test, and when the test was over his fortunes were restored. Even without the assumption that the epilogue and prologue are additions, the analysis of Job's answer still stands.

64. Compare the following diverse scholars who all would agree with this basic assessment of Job. Arthur S. Peake, 'Job: The Problem of the Book', *Job* (Century Bible; New York: Henry Frowde, 1905), pp. 9-21; H.H. Rowley, *The Book of Job*, The New Century Bible Commentary (Grand Rapids: Eerdmans, 1976), pp. 20-21; Koch, 'Is There a Doctrine of Retribution in the Old Testament?', *Theodicy in the Old Testament*, pp. 80-82.

65. Considering the failure of all rational theodicies, could this be the only valid theodicy? Berger (*The Sacred Canopy*, pp. 55-57), used the interesting

term *masochism* to describe this type of theodicy, since it entails the negation of self.

66. Compare also Psalm 16.

67. See Martin Buber, 'The Heart Determines: Psalm 73', *Theodicy in the Old Testament*, pp. 109-18; Ronald J. Williams, 'Theodicy in the Ancient Near East', pp. 21-22.

68. See also Sir. 3.26-31; 7.1; etc.

69. See also Jub. 17.17-19.

70. 1 Macc. 3.52; see also Jud. 8.25-27 and Wis. 3.5-6.

71. James L. Crenshaw ('The Problem of Theodicy in Sirach: On Human Bondage', *Theodicy in the Old Testament*, p. 132) traced this idea into Wis. 16.22-24.

72. See Sir. 39.12-35 for the whole argument.

73. O.S. Rankin traced this idea through Augustine to Leibniz. this does indeed sound like Leibniz's 'best of all possible worlds'. See Rankin, *Israel's Wisdom Literature*, p. 34. On this idea of Sirach see also von Rad, *Wisdon in Israel*, p. 254; James L. Crenshaw, 'The Problem of Theodicy in Sirach: On Human Bondage', pp. 129-30.

74. The example given here from the Wisdom of Solomon is only one of many references and forms of this doctrine. See the extensive passages studied in George W.E. Nickelsburg, *Resurrection, Immortality, and Eternal Life in Intertestamental Judaism* (Cambridge, Massachusetts: Harvard University Press, 1972); H.C.C. Cavallin, *Life After Death: Paul's Argument for the Resurrection of the Dead in I Cor. 15*, Part I: An Enquiry into the Jewish Background (Coniectanea Biblica, New Testament Series, 71; Lund: C.W.K. Gleerup, 1974). Both studies came to the same basic conclusion: no matter what forms were used to describe the future world, the common motif was future retribution and final justice. See Nickelsburg, pp. 170-76; Cavallin, pp. 211-14.

Notes to Chapter 2

1. These definitions follow those proposed by the Society of Biblical Literature 1977 Seminar papers published in *Semeia* 14 (1979), *Apocalypse: Towards the Morphology of a Genre*, ed. John J. Collins.

2. Disagreement reigns even over the term *eschatology*. See Hans-Peter Müller, *Ursprünge und Strukturen alttestamentlicher Eschatologie* (Berlin: Töpelmann, 1969), especially pp. 1-7. Following Müller *eschatology* will be used in this book to refer both to the apocalyptic consummation of history and the prophetic vision of the coming new action of Yahweh within history.

3. For example, see Walter Schmithals, *The Apocalyptic Movement*:

Introduction & Interpretation (trans. John E. Steely; Nashville: Abingdon, 1975).

4. For a survey of early research see Johann Michael Schmidt, *Die jüdische Apokalyptik: Die Geschichte ihrer Erforschung von den Anfängen bis zu den Textfunden von Qumran* (2nd edn; Düsseldorf: Neukirchener Verlag, 1976).

5. H.H. Rowley, *The Relevance of Apocalyptic: A Study of Jewish and Christian Apocalypses from Daniel to the Revelation* (Greenwood, S.C.: Attic, 1963); R.H. Charles, ed., *Apocrypha and Pseudepigrapha of the Old Testament*, Vol. II (Oxford: Clarendon, 1913).

6. D.S. Russell, *The Method and Message of Jewish Apocalyptic* (The Old Testament Library; Philadelphia: Westminster, 1964).

7. Ibid., pp. 15-20.

8. Ibid., p. 17.

9. Ibid., p. 16.

10. See Russell, pp. 20-28, 73-103.

11. Ibid., pp. 28-33.

12. Ibid., pp. 104-39.

13. Klaus Koch, *The Rediscovery of Apocalyptic* (trans. Magaret Kohl; Studies in Biblical Theology, 2nd Series, 22; Naperville, Ill.: Allenson, 1970).

14. Koch, pp. 36-48. Koch has presented nothing new concerning the history of scholarship; he has clearly shown the influence this history has had on the study of apocalypticism.

15. Koch (p. 49) points out the parochial nature of both German and English scholarship; both have neglected the research of the other.

16. Ibid., pp. 49-56.

17. See *APOT*, II, pp. vii-xi, for a summary of Charles's thought.

18. See Koch, pp. 57-97, for the fortunes of apocalyptic literature at the hands of New Testament scholarship.

19. Ibid., p. 23.

20. Christopher Rowland, *The Open Heaven: A Study of Apocalyptic in Judaism and Early Christianity* (New York: Crossroad, 1982), pp. 15-16.

21. Ibid., p. 14. The 'all this' refers to the failure of past research to reach agreement.

22. Paul D. Hanson, *The Dawn of Apocalyptic: The Historical and Sociological Roots of Jewish Apocalyptic* (Philadelphia: Fortress, 1975); see e.g. pp. 9-10.

23. Hanson, p. 11.

24. Koch, pp. 11-13.

25. For the German speaking world compare the comment of Otto Plöger (*Theocracy and Eschatology* [trans. S. Rudman; Oxford: Blackwell, 1968], p. 26), 'It is customary to regard the influx of foreign influences, particularly

the adoption of the Iranian dualistic cosmology, as responsible for the birth of apocalyptic eschatology'. This is an accurate assessment for continental research; on the differing views of apocalypticism in the English speaking and German speaking worlds, see above.

26. H.H. Rowley, *The Relevance of Apocalyptic*, p. 15. On the connection between prophecy and apocalypticism see also, George Ricker Berry, 'The Apocalyptic Literature of the Old Testament', *JBL* 62 (1943), pp. 9-16; Joshua Bloch, *On the Apocalyptic in Judaism* (Jewish Quarterly Review Monograph Series, 2; Philadelphia: Dropsie College for Hebrew and Cognate Learning, 1952), especially pp. 28-39; Stanley Brice Frost, *Old Testament Apocalyptic: Its Origins and Growth*, Fernley-Hartley Lecture, 1952 (London: Epworth, 1952); Plöger, *Theocracy and Eschatology*, pp. 26-52; D.S. Russell, *The Method and Message of Jewish Apocalyptic*, especially p. 88; Michael E. Stone, *Scriptures, Sects, and Visions: A Profile of Judaism from Ezra to the Jewish Revolts* (Philadelphia: Fortress, 1980), especially pp. 46-47.

27. See for example Hanson, *The Dawn of Apocalyptic*. Hanson's work was done mainly on the sociological roots of apocalypticism and to this subject we will return later. See also B. Erling, 'Ezekiel 38–39 and the Origins of Jewish Apocalyptic', *Ex Orbe Religionum: Studia Geo Widengren*, Vol. I (Supplements to Numen, 21; Leiden: Brill, 1972); William R. Millar, *Isaiah 24–27 and the Origin of Apocalyptic* (Harvard Semitic Monograph Series, 11; Missoula, Mont.: Scholars Press, 1976).

28. Robert North, 'Prophecy to Apocalyptic via Zechariah', *Supplements to Vetus Testamentum* 22 (Leiden: Brill, 1972), p. 53.

29. On this confusion see note 2 above.

30. See John J. Collins, 'Pseudonymity, Historical Reviews and the Genre of the Revelation of John', *CBQ* 39 (1977), pp. 329-43; G.I. Davies, 'Apocalyptic and Historiography', *JSOT* 5 (1978), pp. 15-28; William R. Murdock, 'History and Revelation in Jewish Apocalyptic', *Int* 21 (1967), pp. 167-87; Martin Noth, 'The Understanding of History in Old Testament Apocalyptic', *The Laws in the Pentateuch and Other Studies* (trans. D.R. Ap-Thomas; Edinburgh and London: Oliver & Boyd, 1966), pp. 194-214; Bruce Vawter, 'Apocalyptic: Its Relation to Prophecy', '*CBQ* 22 (1960), pp. 33-46.

31. See Gerhard von Rad, *Old Testament Theology*, II (trans. D.M.G. Stalker; New York: Harper & Row, 1965), pp. 301-15, but especially his expanded comments in the 4th German edition, *Theologie des Alten Testaments* (4th edn; Munich: Kaiser, 1965), II, pp. 316-38.

32. Peter von der Osten-Sacken (*Die Apokalyptik in ihrem Verhältnis zu Prophetie und Weisheit* [München: Kaiser, 1969]) wrote specifically to contradict von Rad's conclusions. Even though he would admit a later wisdom influence, he insisted on the prophetic-apocalyptic connection.

33. For example, John J. Collins, 'The Court-Tales in Daniel and the Development of Apocalyptic', *JBL* 94 (1975), pp. 218-34; George W. E. Nickelsburg, 'The Apocalyptic Message of I Enoch 92–105', *CBQ* 39 (1977), pp. 309-28; both of whom admit varying degrees of influence from both prophecy and wisdom.

34. Hans-Peter Müller, 'Mantische Weisheit und Apokalyptik', *Supplements to Vetus Testamentum* 22 (Leiden: Brill, 1972), pp. 268-93.

35. Arthur S. Peake, 'The Roots of Hebrew Prophecy and Jewish Apocalyptic', *BJRL* 7 (1923), pp. 233-55; S.H. Hooke, 'The Myth and Ritual Pattern in Jewish and Christian Apocalyptic', *The Labyrinth: Further Studies in the Relation between Myth and Ritual in the Ancient World* (London: SPCK, 1935), pp. 211-33.

36. See e.g. J.J. Collins, 'The Court-Tales in Daniel and the Development of Apocalyptic', pp. 231-33.

37. Hans Dieter Betz, 'On the Problem of the Religio-Historical Understanding of Apocalypticism', *JTC* 6 (1969), p. 137.

38. See for example, Wilhelm Bousset, *Die Religion des Judentums im späthellenistischen Zeitalter* (ed. H. Gressmann; 3rd edn, Tübingen: Mohr, 1926), pp. 242-86.

39. On Egyptian influences see C.C. McCown, 'Hebrew and Egyptian Apocalyptic Literature', *HTR* 18 (1925), pp. 357-411. On Canaanite influences see below.

40. Martin Noth, 'The Understanding of History in Old Testament Apocalyptic', pp. 201-203.

41. Sigmund Mowinckel, *He That Commeth* (trans. G.W. Anderson; Nashville: Abingdon, 1954), p. 125.

42. William R. Murdock, 'History and Revelation in Jewish Apocalyptic', pp. 169-71. Otto Plöger (*Theocracy and Eschatology*, pp. 47-49) came to basically the same conclusion.

43. Betz, 'On the Problem of the Religio-Historical Understanding of Apocalypticism', p. 136. He is not alone in this judgment; compare also Jonathan Z. Smith, 'Wisdon and Apocalyptic', *Religious Syncretism in Antiquity: Essays in Conversation with Geo Widengren*, ed. Birger A. Pearson (Missoula, Mont.: Scholars Press, 1975), p. 131; John J. Collins, 'Jewish Apocalyptic against its Hellenistic Near Eastern Environment', *BASOR* 220 (1975), pp. 27-36.

44. S.B. Frost, *Old Testament Apocalyptic*, p. 233.

45. Paul D. Hanson, *The Dawn of Apocalyptic*, pp. 8-9; Frank Moore Cross, *Canaanite Myth and Hebrew Epic: Essays in the History of the Religion of Israel* (Cambridge, Massachusetts: Harvard University Press, 1973), p. 346.

46. Betz, 'On the Problem of the Religio-Historical Understanding of Apocalypticism', p. 138; and a similar conclusion by Christopher Rowland, *The Open Heaven*, p. 196.

47. John J. Collins, 'Jewish Apocalyptic against its Hellenistic Near Eastern Environment', p. 34; Betz, ibid., p. 136; Jonathan Z. Smith, 'Wisdom and Apocalyptic', p. 131.

48. Several of these proposals will be examined below. For a more complete list see Koch, *The Rediscovery of Apocalyptic*, p. 21; Rowland, *The Open Heaven*, pp. 199-247; or Russell, *The Method and Message of Jewish Apocalyptic*, pp. 15-33.

49. Plöger, *Theocracy and Eschatology*, pp. 106-17.

50. Frank Moore Cross, *The Ancient Library of Qumran and Modern Biblical Studies*, The Haskell Lectures, 1956-1957 (Garden City, N.Y.: Doubleday, 1958), pp. 98-100, 147; see also K. Kohler, 'The Essenes and the Apocalyptic Literature', *JQR* 11 (1920), pp. 145-68.

51. On concerns reflecting an upper class point of view, see Bo Reicke, 'Official and Pietistic Elements of Jewish Apocalypticism', *JBL* 79 (1960), pp. 137-50; see also R.G. Hamerton-Kelly, 'The Temple and the Origins of Jewish Apocalyptic', *VT* 20 (1970), pp. 1-15.

52. See e.g. Louis Ginzberg, 'Some Observations on the Attitude of the Synagogue towards the Apocalyptic-Eschatological Writings', *JBL* 41 (1922), p. 136; Michael A. Knibb, 'Apocalyptic and Wisdom in 4 Ezra', *JSJ* 13 (1982), pp. 56-74; on von Rad, see note 30 above.

53. For a short summary of his views, see R.H. Charles, 'Introduction to Volume II', *APOT*, II, pp. vii-xi.

54. For a reasonable and fair treatment of Charles, see Kohler, 'The Essenes and the Apocalyptic Literature', pp. 145-68.

55. On the relationship to legalistic Judaism, see below on Rabbis and apocalypticism. The apocalypses have been accused of having no ethical content. This lack casts doubt on the apocalyptic-prophetic connection since the prophets were the founders of '*ethical* monotheism'. On the ethical content see H. Maldwyn Hughes, *The Ethics of Jewish Apocryphal Literature* (London: Robert Culley, n.d.); R. Travers Herford, *Talmud and Apocrypha: A Comparative Study of the Jewish Ethical Teaching in the Rabbinical and non-Rabbinical Sources in the Early Centuries* (London: Soncino, 1933), ch. 2; for the discussion about the ethical content see Russell, pp. 100-103.

56. Ginzberg, 'The Attitude of the Synagogue', pp. 115-36; to further support his argument he also tried to show that the Rabbis were the true heirs of the prophets. See also F. Crawford Burkitt, *Jewish and Christian Apocalypses*, The Schweich Lectures, 1913 (London: Oxford University Press, 1914), pp. 12-16.

57. See Bloch, *On The Apocalyptic in Judaism*, pp. 70-73, 82-85, 89-111; Rowland, *The Open Heaven*, pp. 271-348, for the arguments.

58. Besides Russell, p. 27, see, David Noel Freedman, 'The Flowering of Apocalyptic', *JTC* 6 (1969), p. 169; Hanson, *The Dawn of Apocalyptic*, p. 20.

59. Paul Hanson, *The Dawn of Apocalyptic*, pp. 9-10.

60. See Hanson, p. 20, for his rejection of the party approach.

61. This has usually been a legalistic stream and a prophetic -apocalyptic stream.

62. On Charles's two types of Pharisaism see pp. 37-38 above; on Russell's two strands, see pp. 36-37 above; see also Plöger, *Theocracy and Eschatology*, who suggested theocratic and apocalyptic strands.

63. Stone, *Scriptures, Sects and Visions*, p. 43.

64. Besides those listed above, see Freedman, 'The Flowering of Apocalyptic', p. 173.

65. Compare Murdock, 'History and Revelation in Jewish Apocalyptic', pp. 181-82, who asserted that the visions were literary creations and not genuine; and Mathias Rissi, *Time and History. A Study on the Revelation* (trans. Gordon C. Winsor; Richmond, Virginia: John Knox, 1966), pp. 18-21, who asserted tthe opposite for Revelation.

66. Russell, *The Method and Message of Jewish Apocalyptic*, pp. 104-39. Russell's caution is evident in his classification of the list of J. Lindblom (transcendentalism, mythology, cosmological survey, pessimistic historical surveys, dualism, division of time into periods, teaching of Two Ages, numerology, pseudo-ecstasy, artificial claims to inspiration, pseudonymity, and esotericism) as of a more 'incidental nature', p. 105.

67. Hanson (*The Dawn of Apocalyptic*, p. 11) seemed to reject the definition of apocalypticism as a literary form just because of the composite nature (see quotation on p. 45 above); whereas Koch (*The Rediscovery of Apocalyptic*, p. 27) said the composite nature demands form criticism.

68. Compare the argument about Revelation between James Kallas and B. Jones. Kallas ('The Apocalypse—An Apocalyptic Book?', *JBL* 86 [1967], pp. 69-80), assuming the listing definition, argued that Revelation was not apocalyptic because it did not fit the lists. He then proposed a new definition with the attitude toward suffering as the criterion. Jones ('More about the Apocalypse as Apocalyptic', *JBL* 87 [1968], pp. 325-27) pointed out the weaknesses in Kallas's argument and then suggested that the real reason that Revelation is not apocalyptic is its lack of pseudonymity.

69. Besides Jones (ibid.), see Collins, 'Pseudonymity, Historical Reviews and the Genre of Revelation of John', pp. 330-32, who found lack of pseudonymity insufficient to disqualify Revelation as an apocalypse.

70. John J. Collins, *Introduction: Apocalypse. Towards the Morphology of a Genre, Semeia* 14 (1979), p. 9. They further suggested some categories of apocalypses. Type I are characterized by an other-worldly journey; type II do not have an other-worldly journey. Each type has three sub-types: a historical overview, cosmic-political eschatology, or personal eschatology.

71. For the complete report see *Semeia* 14 (1979).

72. Hanson, *The Dawn of Apocalyptic*, pp. 1-11.

73. Rowland, *The Open Heaven*, p. 14.

74. This may be a reaction to the deprecation of the apocalypses, particularly in continental research. Most denials that Revelation is an apocalypse seem intent on this same thing. See, besides Kallas and Jones mentioned in note 65 above, Rissi, *Time and History*, pp. 18-21.

75. Note how Murdock ('History and Revelation in Jewish Apocalyptic', p. 184) described the *Gattung* of the apocalypses in almost the same way: 'The *Gattung* apocalypse may be defined as a reading revelation, a book of divine wisdom in which the mysteries and secrets of God were unfolded before the reader's eyes as he experienced the visions, dreams, and celestial journeys described by the apocalypticist'. The major difference appears to be in the judgment about the reality of the vision.

76. Rowland, *The Open Heaven*, pp. 15-16; he also used it in his search for roots (pp. 199-200).

Notes to Chapter 3

1. Compare the tables showing the various names by Bruce M. Metzger, 'The Fourth Book of Ezra: A New Translation and Introduction', *OTP*, I, p. 516; Nigel Turner, 'Esdras, Books of', *IDB*, II, p. 141.

2. For additional comments see: Robert L. Bensly, *The Fourth Book of Ezra: With an Introduction by Montague Rhodes James*, Texts and Studies, III/2 (Cambridge, Massachusetts: Harvard University Press, 1895), pp. xxiv-xxvii; Jacob M. Myers, *I and II Esdras: Introduction, Translation and Commentary* (Anchor Bible, 42; Garden City, N.Y.: Doubleday, 1974), pp. 107-13.

3. See the following section on original language for the reasons for this judgment.

4. A. Frederik J. Klijn, ed., *Der Lateinische Text der Apokalypse des Esra* (Texte und Untersuchungen zur Geschichte der altchristlichen Literatur, 131; Berlin: Akademie, 1983). Two other important editions of the Latin text are the edition by Bensly, *The Fourth Book of Ezra*, and Bruno Violet, *Die Ezra-Apokalypse (IV Ezra), I. Teil: Die Überlieferung* (Die griechischen christlichen Schriftsteller der ersten drei Jahrhunderte, 18; Leipzig, 1910).

5. R.J. Bidawid, ed., *The Old Testament in Syriac According to the Peshitta Version*, Part IV/3, Apocalypse of Baruch, 4 Esdras (Leiden: Brill, 1973).

6. August Dillmann, *Veteris Testamenti Aethiopici*, Vol. V, Libri apocryphi (Berlin, 1894). A German translation is available in Bruno Violet, *Die Ezra-Apokalypse (IV Esra), I. Teil: Die Überlieferung*.

7. Michael E. Stone, *The Armenian Version of IV Ezra* (University of Pennsylvania Armenian Texts and Studies, 1; Missoula, Mont.: Scholars

Press, 1979). On the value of the Armenian version see Stone, 'Some Remarks on the Textual Criticism of IV Ezra', *HTR* 60 (1967), pp. 107-15, and 'Manuscripts and Readings of Armenian IV Ezra', *Textus* 6 (1968), pp. 48-61.

8. Bruno Violet, *Die Ezra-Apokalypse (IV Ezra), I. Teil: Die Überlieferung*; see p. xxxix for details about the Arabic texts. On a new Arabic text see Michael E. Stone, 'A New Manuscript of the Syrio-Arabic Version of the Fourth Book of Exra', *JSJ* 8 (1977), pp. 183-96.

9. See the evidence offered by Violet, *Die Ezra-Apokalypse (IV Ezra)*, I. Teil, pp. xiii-xxi, *Die Apokalypsen des Esra und des Baruch in deutscher Gestalt* (Leipzig: Hinrichs, 1924), pp. xi-xiii. The one major dissenting voice against Greek underlying the versions is Joshua Bloch, 'Was There a Greek Version of the Apocalpyse of Ezra?', *JQR* 46 (1955/1956), pp. 309-20; and 'The Ezra-Apocalypse: Was It Written in Hebrew, Greek or Aramaic?', *JQR* 48 (1957/1958) pp. 279-94. Leon Gry, *Les dires prophétiques d'Esdras (IV Esdras)*, Vol. I (Paris: Geuthner, 1938), pp. xviii-xxvi, upon whom Bloch relied, argued that the translators of the various versions had a Semitic as well as a Greek original at their disposal.

10. Julius Wellhausen, *Skizzen und Vorarbeiten*, Heft 6 (Berlin: Reimer, 1899), pp. 234-40.

11. Julius Wellhausen, *Einleitung in die drei ersten Evangelien* (Berlin: Reimer, 1911), p. 25 n. 1.

12. Leon Gry, *Les dires prophétiques d'Esdras (IV Esdras)*, I, pp. xviii-xxvi.

13. See especially Stone, 'Some Remarks on the Textual Criticism of IV Ezra', pp. 109-11, for the criticism of Gry.

14. For example, Hermann Gunkel, 'Das vierte Buch Esra', *APAT*, II; G.H. Box, 'IV Ezra', *APOT*, pp. 547-49, Stone, 'Manuscripts and Readings of Armenian IV Ezra', p. 48, and the work of Armand Kaminka, 'Beiträge zur Erklärung der Esra-Apokalypse und zur Rekonstruktion ihres hebräischen Urtextes', *Monatsschrift für Geschichte und Wissenschaft des Judentums* 76 (1932), pp. 121-38, 206-12, 494-511, 604-607; 77 (1933), pp. 339-55. The matter is not decided, however; note the recent cautious statement of Klijn, *Der lateinische Text der Apokalypse des Esra*, p. 11, 'Diese Liste gibt eine Auswahl wichtiger Stellen, die eine Urform beweisen dürften, die im grossen und ganzen als hebräische betrachtet werden kann, doch auch einen aramäischen Einfluss aufweist'.

15. Frank Zimmermann, 'Underlying Documents of IV Ezra', *JQR* 51 (1960/1961), pp. 107-34.

16. For a good summary of the various arguments concerning the dating see Jacob M. Myers, *I and II Esdras*, pp. 129-31, 299-302.

17. 4 Ezra 3.2; 6.19; 10.48, etc. are the basis for this judgment.

18. Myers, *I and II Esdras*, p. 301.

19. Leon Vaganay, *Le Problème eschatologique dans le IVe Livre d'Esdras* (Paris: Picard, 1906), pp. 15-23.

20. For example, Joseph Keulers, *Die eschatologische Lehre des vierten Esrabuches* (Berlin: Herder, 1922), p. 108; Gustav Volkmar, *Handbuch der Einleitung in die Apokryphen: Zweite Abteilung, Das vierte Buch Esra* (Tübingen: Fues, 1863), pp. 368-69; Violet, *Die Ezra-Apokalypse (IV Ezra)*, II, p. 1.

21. For example, Gunkel, 'Das vierte Buch Esra', p. 352; Box, 'IV Ezra', *APOT*, pp. 552-53; Bloch, 'The Ezra-Apocalypse', p. 282.

22. The categories of Box, *The Ezra-Apocalypse, Being Chapters 3-14 of the Book Commonly Known as 4 Ezra (or II Esdras)* (London: Pitman, 1912), pp. xxi-xxxiii, are used in the following description. See the similar analyses of Richard Kabisch, *Das vierte Buch Esra auf seine Quellen untersucht* (Göttingen: Vandenhoeck & Ruprecht, 1889); W.O.E. Oesterley, *II Esdras (the Ezra Apocalypse): With an Introduction and Notes* (Westminster Commentaries; London: Methuen, 1933), pp. xi-xix.

23. Gunkel, 'Das vierte Buch Esra', pp. 331-52. Egon Brandenburger, *Die Verborgenheit Gottes im Weltgeschehen. Das literarische und theologische Problem des 4. Esrabuches* (Abhandlungen zur Theologie des Alten und Neuen Testaments, 68; Zürich: Theologischer Verlag, 1981), pp. 91-139, has given the most recent and most detailed defense of the unity of the book; see also Gry, *Les dires prophétiques d'Esras (IV Esdras)*, Vol. I, pp. cxiii-cxxiv; Myers, *I and II Esdras*, pp. 119-21.

24. Gunkel, 'Das vierte Buch Esra', p. 343. W. Mundle, 'Das religiöse Problem des IV Esrabuches', *ZAW* 47 (1929), pp. 222-49, criticized Gunkel for too easily assuming that Ezra represented the author's viewpoint.

25. Keulers (*Die eschatologische Lehre des vierten Esrabuches*, pp. 11-55) was the first to work out this thought in detail. Violet in his commentary, *Die Apokalypsen des Esra und des Baruch in deutscher Gestalt* (Leipzig: Hinrichs, 1924) also followed this approach.

26. The suggestion was made in Brandenburger, *Adam und Christus. Exegetisch-religionsgeschichtliche Untersuchung zu Röm. 5.12-21 (1 Kor. 15)* (WMANT, 7; Neukirchen-Vluyn: Neukirchener Verlag, 1962), p. 30, and followed by Harnisch in *Verhängnis und Verheissung der Geschichte. Untersuchungen zum Zeit- und Geschichtsverständnis im 4. Buch Esra und in der syr. Baruchapokalypse* (Göttingen: Vandenhoeck & Ruprecht, 1969), pp. 63-64, and followed by Brandenburger in *Die Verborgenheit Gottes im Weltgeschehen*.

27. For a critique of Harnisch, see A.P. Hayman, 'The Problem of Pseudonymity in the Ezra Apocalypse', *JSJ* 6 (1975), pp. 50-51.

28. Volkmar, *Handbuch der Einleitung in die Apokryphen*.

29. Brandenburger, *Die Verborgenheit Gottes im Weltgeschehen*, pp. 95-98, with the examples removed, this author's translation.

30. Brandenburger (p. 95) acknowledged his debt to Harnisch for the analysis of the first four sections.

31. Even though he characterized the fasts as preparation for a revelation, perhaps on the basis of 5.13 and 6.31, a revelation does not follow immediately. Note also how in sections 5-7, which do begin with a revelation, the fast is missing from the list, and only in 12.51 could it be implied. A lament, however, does accompany the fast in 5.20 and 6.35.

32. In the following analysis the internal narrative links are listed as part of the unit to which they are tied.

33. This grouping is indebted to Alden L. Thompson, *Responsibility for Evil in the Theodicy of IV Ezra: A Study Illustrating the Significance of Form and Structure for the Meaning of the Book* (Society of Biblical Literature Dissertation Series, 29; Missoula, Mont.: Scholars Press, 1977), pp. 122-24; compare also the study of 2 Baruch in the following chapter of this book.

34. This group could include many sub-unit prayers within larger units such as dialogues, for example 8.4-36. In this analysis only the prayers which function outside these other literary units will be noted.

35. Within the dialogues in the first four sections are other literary units, such as the prayer mentioned in the previous footnote and the lament in 7.62-69. Also included within this category are the interpretations of the visions, 10.29-59, etc.

36. Box (*The Ezra-Apocalypse*, pp. 4-6), following Kabisch (*Das vierte Buch Esra*, pp. 131-43), concluded, probably correctly, that the original introduction to the book has been lost. What remains here is a shortened version.

37. See Thompson, *Responsibility for Evil in the Theodicy of IV Ezra*, especially pp. 332-39, for the *yeṣer* tradition in relation to the evil heart in 4 Ezra.

38. 4 Ezra 3.20. This and the following quotations from 4 Ezra were taken from the translation of Bruce Metzger, 'The Fourth Book of Ezra', *OTP* I, pp. 514-59.

39. 4 Ezra 3.31b.

40. 4 Ezra 4.12.

41. The angel, after attempting to persuade Ezra that he is unable to understand the things about which he is asking because they concerned the things of heaven, ironically tries to turn Ezra's attention to the esoteric knowledge of the future.

42. This analogy further shows the parallel nature of these first two sections; compare this to the analogy in the preceding section (4.40).

43. 4 Ezra 5.56. The change of subject matter began at 5.50, but 5.56 clearly signaled the change. The introduction of the one 'through whom' God is going to visit his creation is abrupt. Box ('IV Ezra', *APOT*, p. 574) may be correct seeing a polemical intent behind the passage.

44. 4 Ezra 6.59.
45. 4 Ezra 7.14.
46. 4 Ezra 7.18a.
47. 4 Ezra 7.18b.
48. Thompson (*Responsibility for Evil in the Theodicy of IV Ezra*, pp. 188-218) gives a good analysis of how this new element changes the direction of the entire argument. On this change see also the analysis of the theodicy below.
49. 4 Ezra 8.3.
50. 4 Ezra 10.16; see also 9.24. (The phrase in brackets was apparently inadvertently omitted in the printing of the text in *OTP*.)
51. 4 Ezra 12.8.
52. 4 Ezra 13.20.
53. 4 Ezra 13.57-58. E.P. Sanders (*Paul and Palestinian Judaism: A Comparison of Patterns of Religion* [Philadelphia: Fortress, 1977], pp. 416-18) argued that the visions in sections V and VI come from the hand of the final redactor and not the author of 4 Ezra. He makes this judgment by insisting that the author's point of view is represented by the angel. The following analysis of the theodicy argument will show that the author's view is not so easily found.
54. Box, 'IV Ezra', *APOT*, p. 542.
55. Gunkel, 'Das vierte Buch Esra', p. 348.
56. Except perhaps in 14.14-15.
57. Earl Breech, in his influential article on 4 Ezra, 'These Fragments I Have Shored Against My Ruins: The Form and Function of 4 Ezra', *JBL* 92 (1973), p. 270, has glossed over the differences between the first three sections too much, especially section three.
58. If one takes seriously the structure of the book then many of the problems in understanding it can be resolved. If as suggested here, sections I and II present the problem which the book attempts to resolve, then the form of the problem presented in them is the major problem the book addresses. Thus much of the confusion Thompson, *Responsibility for Evil*, pp. 259-67, found over whether the problem is present distress or future judgment is resolved.
59. 4 Ezra 3.1b-2.
60. 4 Ezra 5.40.
61. 4 Ezra 6.27-28.
62. 4 Ezra 6.26b.
63. 4 Ezra 6.59.
64. Gunkel (*APAT*, p. 343) pointed out how the author, at 7.16, changed from considering the problems of the present age to the problems of the future age.
65. 4 Ezra 7.18.

66. 4 Ezra 7.46, compare also 7.68.
67. Harnisch (*Verhängnis und Verheissung*, pp. 42-58) reached a similar conclusion.
68. Thompson (*Responsibility for Evil*, pp. 267-69) argued that the author of 4 Ezra had a strong universalistic concern behind the argument, especially as found in section III. If, however, the reason for Ezra's concern for the wicked is his realization that all, including the Israelites, are sinners, then Ezra's concern for the wicked is nothing more than a natural extension of his concern for Israel.
69. 4 Ezra 8.35.
70. Box (*The Ezra-Apocalypse*, p. xxxix) noted this but attributed it solely to S.
71. 4 Ezra 8.36.
72. 4 Ezra 8.41.
73. 4 Ezra 8.45.
74. 4 Ezra 9.15-16. Box (*The Ezra-Apocalypse*, p. 205) noted the salvation by mercy alone at this point.
75. Thompson (*Responsibility for Evil*, pp. 229-32), went to great lengths to find the change in Ezra and his theodicy at 10.16-17. Significant as this passage is, it only represents the change which has already been wrought, but Thompson's analysis of the literary artistry used in this vision to communicate the theodicy is undoubtedly correct.
76. 4 Ezra 9.36.
77. 4 Ezra 9.37.
78. 4 Ezra 10.24.
79. 4 Ezra 14.58.
80. Leon Vaganay, *Le Problème eschatologique dans le IVe livre d'Esdras* (Paris: Picard, 1906).
81. Ibid., p. 60.
82. Keulers, *Die eschatologische Lehre des vierten Esrabuches*. Keulers, though he noted Vaganay's study, gave little attention to it in his own.
83. Keulers (p. 46) was aware of the difficulties encountered in trying to separate the two types of eschatology.
84. Most of the older commentators gave an elaborate scheme for analyzing the eschatology in 4 Ezra. Box (*APOT*, II, pp. 554-59), for example, found an eschatology of the individual in 4.22-43, and a national eschatology in 4.51–5.13. Box could make such a distinction, however, only on the basis of his source analysis: 4.22-43 was attributed to S which *always* presented an individual eschatology and 4.51–5.13 was attributed to E which presented a national eschatology. The material itself, however, does not support such a distinction. Only out of context could 4.22-43 be construed as speaking of an individual eschatology. Compare the analysis of Thompson,

Responsibility for Evil, pp. 157-256, especially pp. 188-217, who argued that Ezra's concern until section III was exclusively national.

85. Michael E. Stone ('The Concept of the Messiah in IV Ezra', *Religions in Antiquity: Essays in Memory of Erwin Ramsdell Goodenough* [Supplements to Numen, 14; ed. Jacob Neusner; Leiden: Brill, 1968], pp. 295-312) was surely correct when he insisted that the meaning of a vision is contained within the interpretation of the vision and not the vision itself, since the vision itself may have come from tradition, but the interpretation comes from the author. Without the interpretation, the eagle vision presents a purely political/this-worldly eschatology, but the interpretation subsumes this concept under the larger rubric by mentioning the end of the Messianic reign and the last judgment.

86. Ibid., p. 312.

87. 4 Ezra 14.35.

88. Samuel S. Cohen ('Original Sin', *Hebrew Union College Annual* 21 [1948], p. 298) called Ezra's solution 'dangerously' close to Pauline thought.

Notes to Chapter 4

1. The terminology 'distress-consolation' is borrowed from an article by Earl Breech, 'These Fragments I have Shored Against My Ruins: The form and Function of 4 Ezra', *JBL* 92 (1973), pp. 267-74, and is also used by Gwendolyn B. Sayler, *Have the Promises Failed? A Literary Analysis of 2 Baruch* (Society of Biblical Literature Dissertation Series, 72; Chico, Ca.: Scholars Press, 1984).

2. MS B.21 Inf., fols. 257a-265b, in the Ambrosian Library at Milan.

3. Three of these are from two British Museum MSS: BM Add. 14.686 and 14.687; on these see W. Baars, 'Neue Textzeugen der syrischen Baruchapokalypse', *VT* 13 (1963), pp. 476-78. The fourth excerpt, Pampakuda [in Kerala, India] A. Konath Library, MS 77, was first pointed out by S. Dedering, ed., *The Old Testament in Syriac According to the Peshitta Version*, Part IV/3, Apocalypse of Baruch, 4 Esdras (Leiden: Brill, 1973), p. iii.

4. On this manuscript see P. Sj. Van Konigsveld, 'An Arabic Manuscript of the Apocalypse of Baruch', *JSJ* 6 (1975), pp. 205-207. Konigsveld concluded that the Arabic manuscript was not a direct translation of *Bibliotheca Ambrosiana*.

5. See R.H. Charles, ed., *APOT*, II, p. 472, for an evaluation of the fragment, and pp. 487-90 for a copy of this fragment in parallel columns with the translation.

6. See Pierre Bogaert, *Apocalypse de Baruch, introduction, traduction du Syriaque et commentaire*, Vol. I (Sources Chrétiennes, 144; Paris: Cerf, 1969), pp. 67-78, for a discussion of the manuscript evidence of the letter.

7. A.M. Ceriani, ed., 'Apocalypsis Syriace Baruch', *Monumenta Sacra et Profana*, Vol. V/2 (Mediolani: Bibliotheca Ambrosiana, 1871), pp. 113-80.
8. M. Kmosko, *Epistola Baruch filli Neriae*, Patrologia Syriaca, I/2 (Paris: Firmin-Didot, 1907), cols. 1056-1236.
9. S. Dedering, ed., *The Old Testament in Syriac According to the Peshitta Version*, pp. 1-50.
10. R.H. Charles, *The Apocalypse of Baruch: With an Introduction by W.O.E. Oesterley* (London: SPCK, 1918): *idem*, *APOT*, II, pp. 470-526.
11. Pierre Bogaert, *Apocalypse de Baruch, introduction, traduction du Syriaque et commentaire.*
12. A.F.J. Klijn, 'Die syrische Baruch-Apokalypse', *Jüdische Schriften aus hellenistisch-römischer Zeit*, Part 5/2 (Gütersloh: Gerd Mohn, 1976); *idem*, '2 (Syriac Apocalypse of) Baruch: A new Translation and Introduction', *OTP*, I, pp. 615-52.
13. *APOT*, II, pp. 471-74; Louis Ginzberg, 'Apocalypse of Baruch (Syriac)', *Jewish Encyclopedia* (1902), Vol. II, pp. 551-56; Bruno Violet, *Die Apokalypsen des Esra und des Baruch in deutscher Gestalt* (Leipzig: Hinrichs, 1924). A modern proponent of this view is Frank Zimmermann, 'Textual Observations on the Apocalypse of Baruch', *JTS* 40 (1939), pp. 151-56.
14. Pierre Bogaert, *Apocalypse de Baruch*, I, pp. 353-80.
15. This quotation from 2 Baruch and those that follow in this chapter are from Klijn's translation cited earlier.
16. For a discussion of the various dating proposals see Sayler, *Have the Promises Failed? A Literary Analysis of 2 Baruch*, pp. 103-110; Bogaert, *Apocalypse de Baruch, introduction, traduction du Syriaque et commentaire*, I, pp. 270-94; and the sources they cite.
17. Bogaert, *Apocalypse de Baruch*, I, 348.
18. Sayler, *Have the Promises Failed?*, p. 115.
19. See Bogaert, *Apocalypse de Baruch*, I, 67-72, for the differing Syriac manuscript traditions.
20. Ibid., pp. 72-73.
21. Konigsveld, 'An Arabic Manuscript of the Apocalypse of Baruch', p. 206.
22. Bogaert, *Apocalypse de Baruch*, I, 78.
23. Sayler, *Have the Promises Failed?*, pp. 98-101.
24. Bogaert, *Apocalypse de Baruch*; Sayler, *Have the Promises Failed?*
25. This grouping and the following are dependent on Sayler, *Have the Promises Failed?*, p. 13, with a few variations which are noted.
26. 10.6-19 is the only proper lament. 11.1–12.4 is a pronouncement (almost a curse) on Babylon. Bogaert (*Apocalypse de Baruch*, I, p. 65), groups 11.1–12.4 with the lament proper, whereas Sayler (*Have the Promises Failed?*, p. 13) labels 12.1-4 as a discourse.
27. Sayler (*Have the Promises Failed?*, p. 13) labels this a conversation, but

it is a strange conversation. Baruch never directly addresses Ramael. The only possible place Baruch might be addressing Ramael is ch. 75, but this resembles a prayer, as noted earlier.

28. Sayler (*Have the Promises Failed?*, p. 13) labeled the first vision (6.4–8.2) part of a narrative unit; Bogaert (*Apocalypse de Baruch*, I, p. 65) classified it a vision. Even though *vision* (*ḥzy'*) does not introduce the first vision as it does the second and third visions, *ḥz'*, the normal semitic word for seeing a vision, does.

29. Bogaert, *Apocalypse de Baruch*, I, pp. 59-60.

30. Sayler, *Have the Promises Failed?*, p. 12.

31. Note, however, that in 5.7 the fast only lasts one day.

32. Sayler (*Have the Promises Failed?*, p. 14) listed three basic concerns: 'How will Israel survive? What will be the future of the world? Are God's words to Moses about Israel still efficacious?' The second and last questions are a different way of stating the same concern; the second question appeals to the belief that the world was created for Israel and asks if the world will also be destroyed now that Israel will be no more; the last question appeals to the promises made to Moses and suggests that the destruction of Jerusalem will go against the promises made to Moses.

33. Bogaert, *Apocalypse de Baruch*, I, pp. 58-67.

34. Charles (*APOT*, II, p. 483) agreed with this and all the other break points proposed here except for the placing of the fasts with the following sections. The other scholars did not consistently break either before or after the fasts; in this matter, compare Bogaert who placed the fast at the end of his first section (12.5) whereas he placed the fast at the beginning of his fifth section (47.2).

35. Bogaert (*Apocalypse de Baruch*, I, p. 59) also considered the fasts preparation for a revelation.

36. Sayler (*Have the Promises Failed?*, p. 15) also placed the break between the first and second sections at the end of ch. 5, recognizing the introductory function of the section, citing the unified character of the content, but placing the major weight on the time reference: 'we sat there and fasted till evening' (5.7).

37. Bogaert, *Apocalypse de Baruch*, I, 58-67. The clearest break according to Bogaert's criteria is between chs. 9 and 10, where a change of place, a seven-day fast, and the people all converge.

38. Sayler (*Have the Promises Failed?*, p. 16) recognized the connection between the first and second sections, but failed to include that in her data when analyzing the break between the sections.

39. 2 Bar. 9.2.

40. Sayler, *Have the Promises Failed?*, p. 17.

41. See 1.1; 10.1; 13.2. God is named differently in each place.

42. Sayler (*Have the Promises Failed?*, p. 19) summarized her second

section (which equals sections II–IV here) in much the same words and used the unified theme to support the division. She failed to notice the connections to the first section, however, and the common themes running throughout this whole half.

43. Sayler, *Have the Promises Failed?*, pp. 22-23.

44. Ibid., p. 23. She accused Bogaert of 'artificiality' when he ignored the changes of place, characters, and content which occurred at 31.1 but she has likewise ignored the changes which occur at 35.1.

45. Ibid., p. 22. Even though she admitted the connection of Baruch's speech to the people with the previous dialogue betwen Baruch and God, she chose instead to emphasize the unity of theme between the speech to the people and the following lament. However, the lament is a final response to the destruction of Jerusalem and not directly connected to speech to the people.

46. Compare the people's worry about losing their father in 32.9 to Baruch's complaint about the downfall of his mother at 3.1; also note how the people express a death wish in 33.3 much like Baruch did in 3.2. Sayler (*Have the Promises Failed?*, p. 25) pointed out this parallel.

47. Ibid., p. 24.

48. Sayler (pp. 25-27), once again going against previous scholarship, concluded the section before Baruch's speech and conversation with the people. The same arguments apply. The criteria of changes in location, characters, and content apply equally well to the break at the end of ch. 47; there she ignored the fast. The speech to the people reflects the issues raised by the vision in ch. 36, how those who are faithful to the Torah will inherit the world to come.

49. See previous note.

50. Sayler, *Have the Promises Failed?*, pp. 32-33.

51. Bogaert, *Apocalypse de Baruch*, I, p. 61; Sayler, *Have the Promises Failed?*, p. 33.

52. Sayler (pp. 35-37) began her last section with this address to the people. In this she was following her previous tendency to begin the sections with Baruch's speeches (31.1; 44.1). She listed parallels in content between ch. 77 and chs. 1–5, showing how the questions raised at the first are answered at the last to unify the section. In spite of these parallels, however, she called the last section an epilogue and considered it not necessary, since all the questions had already been answered. Bogaert (pp. 58-67), breaking with previous scholarship, sugested that 77.1-17 concluded the vision and its interpretation. By doing this, he consistently placed Baruch's speeches to the people and conversations at the last of each respective section. Once again Sayler accused Bogaert of ignoring the changes of place, character, and content between chs. 76 and 77. As with the previous two occasions when Baruch's words to and with the people are recorded (31.1ff.; 44.1ff.), his

words echo the recent encounter with God and naturally continue it. Bogaert judged correctly here.

53. Wolfgang Harnisch (*Verhängnis und Verheissung der Geschichte. Untersuchungen zum Zeit- und Geschichtsverständnis im 4. Buch Esra und in der syr. Baruchapokalyse* [Göttingen: Vandenhoeck & Ruprecht, 1969], p. 80) noted this and described the fate of the individual as the theme of the entire book.

54. 2 Bar. 3.9.

55. This doctrine is close to the doctrine of the remnant found in the Old Testament, particularly in the Isaiah tradition (see Isa. 4.2 ff.; 10.20-22; 11.10-16; 28.5; 37.22 among others). Like the biblical Jeremianic tradition (see Jeremiah 24), however, 2 Baruch does not use the word remnant. Compare 2 Bar. 40.2 where the root *srk* was used to describe the *rest* of the people, when all of the roots used in the Bible to describe the remnant were available (*sh'r, plṭ, shrd, ytr*). This *remnant* is not even called the exiles as in Jeremiah, because Baruch is making a distinction among the exiles. This insight is indebted to the comments of Page H. Kelley from private communications.

56. 2 Bar. 48.29.

57. 2 Bar. 48.30; compare this to Jeremiah 45. The tone in 2 Baruch 48 is different than Jeremiah 45; the judgment in Jeremiah 45 is on 'all flesh', but here only on those who deserve it, and the promise to Baruch in Jeremiah 45 is for earthly life and not the result of merit, but here the promise is for translation to the heavenly sphere and a result of merit.

58. This idea was already hinted at in chs. 17–18.

59. 2 Bar. 52.3.

60. See Chapter 1 n. 7 for this term.

61. The translation of the Syriac word *por'ānā'* with 'retribution' in this passage and following ones is truly justified.

62. Sayler (*Have the Promises Failed?*, pp. 44-47), on the basis of supposed parallels with the Old Testament (cf. Deut. 32.30-36) and passages from other Jewish literature (cf. 2 Macc. 6.12-16), interpreted this passage as meaning that God delays the punishment of the nations so that their sins can pile up and thereby increase their punishment. The emphasis is not on the punishment of the nations but the redemption of the Jewish nation.

63. Sayler (pp. 56-57), as in the previous passage, limited the concept of long-suffering only to the judgment of the wicked, once again referring to 2 Macc. 6.12-16; however, she failed to take account of 2 Bar. 24.2, which directs God's long-suffering toward both the wicked and the righteous.

64. 2 Bar. 24.4.

65. 2 Bar. 30.4-5.

66. 2 Bar. 39.3.

67. 2 Bar. 54.10.

68. 2 Bar. 54.14.
69. 2 Bar. 54.22.
70. R.H. Charles (*Eschatology*: *The Doctrine of a Future Life in Israel, Judaism and Christianity* [New York: Schocken Books, 1963], pp. 1-166) analyzed the whole of eschatology under the rubrics of individual and national, and found their synthesis in the joining of the doctrine of the Messianic kingdom and the doctrine of the resurrection. For 2 Baruch, however, national eschatology seems to be replaced by individual eschatology.
71. On the heavenly Jerusalem, see W. Harnisch, *Verhängnis und Verheissung der Geschichte*, pp. 110-11; Bogaert, *Apocalypse de Baruch*, I, pp. 421-25.
72. 2 Bar. 14.14.
73. 2 Bar. 20.2.
74. Charles rendered this the 'method of the times'. Syriac had *dwbrhwn dzbn'*. Klijn translated *dwbrhwn* in 59.4 as 'ways' and Charles as 'principles'.
75. H.C.C. Cavallin (*Life After Death*: *Paul's Argument for the Resurrection of the Dead in I Cor. 15*. Part I: An Enquiry into the Jewish Background [Coniectanea Biblica, New Testament Series, 7/1; Lund: Gleerup, 1974], pp. 86-94) failed to mention this passage in his otherwise very complete survey.
76. Compare Bogaert, *Apocalypse de Baruch*, I, pp. 416-17; Cavallin, *Life After Death*, p. 86; Charles, *APOT*, II, p. 498.
77. 2 Bar. 30.5; see Cavallin, *Life After Death*, pp. 86-87.
78. 2 Bar. 32.5.
79. This understanding agrees with George W.E. Nickelsburg, *Resurrection, Immortality, and Eternal Life in Intertestamental Judaism* (Cambridge, Mass.: Harvard University Press, 1972), pp. 84-85, who noted that resurrection/exaltation scenes became associated with judgment. Cavallin (*Life After Death*, pp. 89-91) understood the purpose of this first stage of the resurrection as an apology to tell how people could recognize one another after the resurrection. Three things argue against this: (a) nowhere else in 2 Baruch is the concern about recognition after the resurrection mentioned, (b) the first stage happens so that the living can recognize the dead (50.3), not so that the resurrected ones recognize each other, and (c) later the wicked are tormented by the transformation of the righteous (whom they had earlier recognized). Compare Cavallin's comments here to his on 42.7 (p. 91).
80. Note Baruch's speech to the people immediately preceding this passage: 'For that which is now is nothing. But that which is in the future will be very great', (44.8) and the following verses. Also note Baruch's admonition in 52.6 referring to the suffering to be encountered during the tribulation, 'Enjoy yourselves in the suffering which you suffer now'.
81. Once again in opposition to Cavallin, *Life After Death*, pp. 89-91.

Cavallin listed the apologetic intent of this passage as answering a denial or doubt of the resurrection. He made many comparisions to 1 Corinthians 15 where this apologetic intent is explicit (see 15.12 especially). He cited the questions in 2 Baruch 49 as proof for his contention of the apologetic intent, especially the concern about the evil nature of the earthly body ('Will they, perhaps, take again this present form, and will they put on the chained members which are in evil and by which evils are accomplished', 49.3). Nickelsburg (*Resurrection, Immortality, and Eternal Life*, p. 84) also noted the questions in ch. 49, but concluded that a judgment scene was intended.

82. 2 Bar. 74.2.

Notes to Chapter 5

1. See the extensive list of parallel passages in R.H. Charles, *The Apocalypse of Baruch: With an Introduction by W.O.E. Oesterley* (London: SPCK, 1929), pp. 170-71.

2. The parallels in wording and content as mentioned in the previous note are the most vivid literary parallels. These parallels, however, can be misleading when simply listed, because of the differing purposes of the various ideas. The establishment of a literary dependence between the two on the basis of these parallels has so far proven to be futile task.

3. G.H. Box ('IV Ezra', *APOT*, II, p. 553) noted the difference in tone, and attributed it to the influence of different Rabbinic schools. He characterized 2 Baruch as giving what was to become the orthodox position. Compare also F. Rosenthal, *Vier apokryphische Bücher aus der Zeit und Schule R. Akiba's* (Leipzig: Schulze, 1885).

4. Peter Berger, *The Sacred Canopy: Elements of a Sociological Theory of Religion* (Garden City, N.Y.: Doubleday, 1967), p. 74.

5. The different role of the angels in each book is also indicative of the different tone of each book. In 2 Baruch, the angel Ramiel is not introduced until the last section, always before Baruch spoke directly with God. In 4 Ezra, the angel Uriel mediates between God and Baruch until the fifth section, after Ezra's complaints have been answered. Louise Ginzberg ('Some Observations on the Attitude of the Synagogue towards the Apocalyptic-Eschatological Writings', *JBL* 41 [1922], p. 135), commenting on the reason for the introduction of angels in these writings, suggested that '. . . when God commands man can only obey, with an angel one can argue and dispute'.

6. This has led to many declarations that 4 Ezra has a universalistic tendency. See, for example, Claude Goldsmid Montefiore, *IV Ezra: A Study*

in the Development of Universalism (London: George Allen & Unwin, 1929), who used 4 Ezra as a starting place in his discussion of universalism.

7. 2 Bar. 20.2

8. See Chapter 1 (p. 12) for the concept of the rational-irrational continuum.

BIBLIOGRAPHY

Baars, W.,'Neue Textzeugen der syrischen Baruchapokalypse', *VT* 13 (1963), pp. 476-78.

Bailey, J.W., 'The Temporary Messianic Reign in the Literature of Early Judaism', *JBL* 53 (1934), pp. 170-87.

Bensly, Robert L., *The Fourth Book of Ezra: With an Introduction by Montague Rhodes James*, Texts and Studies, 3/2; Cambridge, Mass.: Harvard University Press, 1895.

Berger, Peter L., *The Sacred Canopy: Elements of a Sociological Theory of Religion*, Garden City, N.Y.: Doubleday, 1967.

Berry, George Ricker, 'The Apocalyptic Literature of the Old Testament', *JBL* 62 (1943), pp. 9-16.

Betz, Hans Dieter, 'On the Problem of the Religio-Historical Understanding of Apocalypticism', *JTC* 6 (1969), pp. 134-56.

Bidawid, R.J. ed., *The Old Testament in Syriac According to the Pesitta Version*. IV/3, Apocalypse of Baruch, 4 Esdras, Leiden: Brill, 1973.

Bloch, Joshua, 'The Ezra-Apocalypse: Was It Written in Hebrew, Greek or Aramaic?' *JQR* 48 (1957/58), pp. 279-94.

—*On the Apocalyptic in Judaism*, Jewish Quarterly Review Monograph Series, New Series, 2, Philadelphia: Dropsie College for Hebrew and Cognate Learning, 1952.

—'Some Christological Interpolations in the Ezra-Apocalypse', *HTR* 51 (1958), pp. 87-94.

—'Was There a Greek Version of the Apocalypse of Ezra?', *JQR* 46 (1955/56), pp. 309-20.

Bogaert, Pierre, *Apocalypse de Baruch, introduction, traduction du Syriaque et commentaire*, 2 vols.; Sources Chrétiennes, 144; Paris: Cerf, 1969.

Bousset, D.W. *Die jüdische Apokalyptik, ihre religionsgeschichtliche Herkunft und ihre Bedeutung für das Neue Testament*, Berlin: von Reuther & Reichard, 1903.

Bousset, D. Wilhelm, *Die Religion des Judentums im späthellenistischen Zeitalter*, 3rd edn; ed. Hugo Gressmann; Tübingen: Mohr, 1926.

Box, G.H. and J.I. Landsman, *The Apocalypse of Abraham*, Translations of Early Documents, Series 1, 10; London: SPCK, 1918.

—*The Ezra-Apocalypse, Being Chapters 3-14 of the Book Commonly Known as 4 Ezra (or II Esdras)*, London: Pitman, 1912.

—'IV Ezra', *APOT* II.

Boyarin, D., 'Penitential Liturgy in 4 Ezra', *JSJ* 3 (1972), pp. 30-34.

Brandenburger, Egon, *Adam und Christus. Exegetisch-religions geschichtliche Untersuchung zu Röm. 5.12-21 (1 Kor. 15)*. Wissenschaftliche Monographien zum Alten und Neuen Testament, 7; Neukirchen-Vluyn: Neukirchener Verlag, 1962.

—*Die Verborgenheit Gottes im Weltgeschehen. Das literarische und theologische Problem des 4. Esrabuches*, Abhandlungen zur Theologie des Alten und Neuen Testaments, 68; Zürich: Theologischer Verlag, 1981.

Breech, Earl, 'These Fragments I Have Shored Against My Ruins: The Form and Function of 4 Ezra', *JBL* 92 (1973), pp. 267-74.
Brockington, L.H., *A Critical Introduction to the Apocrypha*, London: Duckworth, 1961.
Buber, Martin, 'The Heart Determines: Psalm 73', *Theodicy in the Old Testament*, ed. James L. Crenshaw; Issues in Religion and Theology, 4; Philadelphia: Fortres, 1983.
Burkitt, F. Crawford, *Jewish and Christian Apocalypses*, The Schweich Lectures, 1913; London: Oxford University Press, 1914.
Cavallin, Hans Clemens Caesarius, *Life After Death: Paul's Argument for the Resurrection of the Dead in I Cor. 15*. Part I: An Enquiry into the Jewish Background; Coniectanea Biblica, New Testament Series, 7/1; Lund: Gleerup, 1974.
Ceriani, A.M., ed., 'Apocalypsis Syriace Baruch', *Monumenta Sacra et Profana*, V/2; Mediolani: Bibliotheca Ambrosiana, 1871.
Charles, R.H., *The Apocalypse of Baruch: With an Introduction by W.O.E. Oesterley*, London: SPCK, 1929.
—ed. *Apocrypha and Pseudepigrapha of the Old Testament*, 2 vols.; Oxford: Clarendon, 1913.
—*Eschatology: The Doctrine of a Future Life in Israel, Judaism, and Christianity*, New York: Schocken Books, 1963.
—*Religious Development between the Old and New Testaments*, London: Williams & Norgate, 1914.
Charlesworth, James H., ed., *The Old Testament Pseudepigrapha: Apocalyptic Literature and Testaments*, Vol. I, Garden City, N.Y.: Doubleday, 1983.
—*The Pseudepigrapha and Modern Research with a Supplement*. Septuagint and Cognate Studies, 7S; Chico, Cal: Scholars Press, 1981.
Cohon, Samuel S., 'Original Sin', *Hebrew Union College Annual* 21 (1948), pp. 275-330.
Collins, Adela Yarboro, 'The History of Religions Approach to Apocalypticism and the 'Angel of the Waters' (Rev. 16.4-7)', *CBQ* 39 (1977), pp. 367-81.
Collins, John J., ed., *Apocalypse: Towards the Morphology of a Genre*, Society of Biblical Literature Seminar Papers, 1977, *Semeia* 14 (1979).
—'Apocalyptic Eschatology as the Transcendence of Death', *CBQ* 36 (1974), pp. 21-43.
—'The Court-Tales in Daniel and the Development of Apocalyptic', *JBL* 94 (1975), pp. 218-34.
—'Jewish Apocalyptic against Its Hellenistic Near Eastern Environment', *BASOR* 220 (1975), pp. 27-36.
—'The Mythology of Holy War in Daniel and the Qumran Scroll: A Point of Transition in Jewish Apocalyptic', *VT* 25 (1975), pp. 596-612.
—'Pseudonymity, Historical Reviews and the Genre of the Revelation of John', *CBQ* 39 (1977), pp. 329-43.
Crenshaw, James L., 'Introduction: The Shift from Theodicy to Anthropodicy', *Theodicy in the Old Testament*, ed. James L. Crenshaw; Issues in Religion and Theology, 4; Philadelphia: Fortress, 1983.
—'Popular Questioning of the Justice of God in Ancient Israel', *ZAW* 82 (1970), pp. 380-95.
—'The Problem of Theodicy in Sirach: On Human Bondage', *Theodicy in the Old*

Testament, ed. James L. Crenshaw; Issues in Religion and Theology, 4; Philadelphia: Fortress, 1983.

—'Theodicy', *IDB, Supplementary Volume.*

Cross, Frank Moore, *The Ancient Library of Qumran and Modern Biblical Studies*, The Haskell Lectures, 1956-1957; Garden City, N.Y.: Doubleday, 1958.

—'Exile and Apocalyptic', *Canaanite Myth and Hebrew Epic: Essays in the History of the Religion of Israel*, Cambridge, Mass.: Harvard University Press, 1973.

Davidson, Robert, *The Courage to Doubt: Exploring an Old Testament Theme*, London: SCM, 1983.

Davies, G.I., 'Apocalyptic and Historiography', *JSOT* 5 (1978), pp. 15-28.

Davies, W.D., *Torah in the Messianic Age and/or the Age to Come*, Journal of Biblical Literature Monograph Series, 7; Philadelphia: Society of Biblical Literature, 1952.

Dedering, S., ed., *The Old Testament in Syriac According to the Peshitta Version*, Part IV/3, Apocalypse of Baruch, 4 Esdras; Leiden: Brill, 1973.

Delling, Gerhard, *Bibliographie zur jüdisch-hellenistischen und intertestamentarischen Literatur 1900-1970*, Texte und Untersuchungen zur Geschichte der altchristlichen Literatur, 106, 2nd edn, Berlin: Akademie, 1975.

De Vries, Simon J., 'Observations on Quantitative and Qualitative Time in Wisdom and Apocalyptic', *Israelite Wisdom: Theological and Literary Essays in Honor of Samuel Terrien*, eds. John G. Gammie, Walter A. Brueggeman, W. Lee Humphreys, and James M. Ward; Missoula, Montana: Scholars Press, 1978.

Dillmann, August, *Veteris Testamenti Aethiopici*, V. Libri apocryphi, Berlin, 1894.

Eichrodt, Walther, 'Faith in Providence and Theodicy in the Old Testament' in *Theodicy in the Old Testament*, ed. James L. Crenshaw; Issues in Religion and Theology, 4; Philadelphia: Fortress, 1983.

— *Theology of the Old Testament*, 2 vols.; trans. J.A. Baker; The Old Testament Library; Philadelphia: Westminster, 1961-1967.

Eissfeldt, Otto, *The Old Testament: An Introduction*, trans. Peter R. Ackroyd; New York: Harper & Row, 1965.

Erling, B., 'Ezekiel 38–39 and the Origins of Jewish Apocalyptic', *Ex Orbe Religionum: Studia Geo Widengren*, Vol I; Supplements to Numen, 21; Leiden: Brill, 1972.

Farrer, Austin, *Love Almighty and Ills Unlimited*, Garden City, N.Y.: Doubleday, 1961.

Fiedler, M.J. 'Dikaiosynē in der diaspora-jüdischen und intertestamentarischen Literatur', *JSJ* 1 (1970), pp. 120-43.

Fiorenza, Elisabeth Schüssler. 'Composition and Structure of the Revelation of John', *CBQ* 39 (1977), pp. 344-66.

Freedman, David Noel, 'The Flowering of Apocalyptic', *JTC* 6 (1969), pp. 166-74.

Fretheim, Terence E., 'Jonah and Theodicy', *ZAW* 90 (1978), pp. 227-37.

Frost, Stanley Brice, 'The Death of Josiah: A Conspiracy of Silence', *JBL* 87 (1968), pp. 367-82.

—*Old Testament Apocalyptic: Its Origins and Growth*, Fernley-Hartley Lecture, 1952; London: Epworth, 1952.

Funk, R.W., ed., 'Apocalypticism', *JTC* 6 (1969).

Gammie, John G., 'The Classification, Stages of Growth, and Changing Intentions in the Book of Daniel', *JBL* 95 (1976), pp. 191-204.

—'The Theology of Retribution in the Book of Deuteronomy', *CBQ* 32 (1970), pp. 1-12.

Gese, Hartmut, 'The Crisis of Wisdom in Koheleth', in *Theodicy in the Old Testament*, ed. James L. Crenshaw; Issues in Religion and Theology, 4; Philadelphia: Fortress, 1983.

Ginzberg, Louis, 'Apocalypse of Baruch (Syriac)', *Jewish Encyclopedia*, 1902, II, pp. 551-56.

—'Some Observations on the Attitude of the Synagogue towards the Apocalyptic-Eschatological Writings', *JBL* 41 (1922), pp. 115-36.

Gordis, Robert, 'A Cruel God or None - Is There No Choice?', *Judaism* 21 (1972), pp. 277-84.

Gowan, Donald E., *The Triumph of Faith in Habakkuk*, Atlanta: John Knox, 1976.

Gray, John, 'The Book of Job in the Context of Near Eastern Literature', *ZAW* 82 (1970), pp. 251-69.

Gry, Leon, 'La Date de la fin des temps', *RB* 48 (1939), pp. 337-56.

—'La "Mort du Messie" en IV Esdras, VII, 29 [III, v. 4]', *Memorial Lagrange*; Paris: Lecoffre, 1940.

—*Les dires prophétiques d'Esdras (IV Esdras)*, 2 vols.; Paris: Geuthner, 1938.

Gunkel, H. *Schöpfung und Chaos*, Göttingen: Vandenhoeck & Ruprecht, 1895.

—'Das vierte Buch Esra', *APAT*, II.

Hadot, Jean. 'Le Problème de l'Apocalypse Syriaque de Baruch d'après un ouvrage récent', *Sem* 20 (1970), pp. 59-76.

Hamerton-Kelly, R.G., 'The Temple and the Origins of Jewish Apocalyptic', *VT* 20 (1970), pp. 1-15.

Hanson, Paul D., *The Dawn of Apocalyptic: The Historical and Sociological Roots of Jewish Apocalyptic*, Philadelphia: Fortress, 1975.

—'Jewish Apocalyptic against its Near Eastern Environment', *RB* 78 (1971), pp. 31-58.

—'Old Testament Apocalyptic Reexamined', *Int* 25 (1971), pp. 454-79.

—'Prolegomena to the Study of Jewish Apocalyptic', *Magnalia Dei: The Mighty Acts of God. Essays on the Bible and Archaeology in Memory of G. Ernest Wright*, eds. Frank Moore Cross, Werner E. Lemke, and Patrick D. Miller, Jr; Garden City, N.Y.: Doubleday, 1976.

Harnisch, Wolfgang, *Verhängnis und Verheissung der Geschichte. Untersuchungen zum Zeit- und Geschichtsverständis im 4. Buch Esra und in der syr. Baruchapokalypse*, Göttingen: Vandenhoeck & Ruprecht, 1969.

Harrelson, Walter, 'Ezra among the Wicked in 2 Esdras 3–10', *The Divine Helmsman: Studies on God's Control of Human Events, Presented to Lou H. Silberman*, ed. James L. Crenshaw and Samuel Sandmel; New York: KTAV, 1980.

Hauer, Chris, Jr, 'When History Stops: Apocalypticism and Mysticism in Judaism and Christianity', *The Divine Helmsman: Studies on God's Control of Human Events, Presented to Lou H. Silberman*, ed. James L. Crenshaw and Samuel Sandmel; New York: KTAV, 1980.

Hayman, A.P., 'The Problem of Pseudonymity in the Ezra Apocalypse', *JSJ* 6 (1975), pp. 45-56.

Herford, R. Travers, *Talmud and Apocrypha: A Comparative Study of the Jewish Ethical Teaching in the Rabbinical and non-Rabbinical Sources in the Early Centuries*, London: Soncino, 1933.

Hick, John, *Evil and the God of Love*, 2nd edn; London: MacMillan, 1977.

Hooke, S.H. 'The Myth and Ritual Pattern in Jewish and Christian Apocalyptic', *The Labyrinth: Further Studies in the Relation between Myth and Ritual in the Ancient World*, London: SPCK, 1935.

Hughes, H. Maldwyn, *The Ethics of Jewish Apocryphal Literature*. London: Robert Culley, n.d.
Hume, David, *Diaglogues Concerning Natural Religion*, ed. Henry D. Aiken; New York: Hafner, 1948.
James, M.R., 'Salathiel qui et Esdras', *JTS* 19 (1918), pp. 347-49.
Jones, Bruce W., 'More about the Apocalypse as Apocalyptic', *JBL* 87 (1968), pp. 325-27.
Kabisch, Richard, *Das vierte Buch Esra auf seine Quellen untersucht*, Göttingen: Vandenhoeck & Ruprecht, 1889.
Kaiser, Otto, *Isaiah 13-39: A Commentary*, trans. R.A. Wilson; The Old Testament Library, Philadelphia: Westminster, 1974.
Kallas, James, 'The Apocalypse - An Apocalyptic Book?', *JBL* 86 (1967), pp. 69-80.
Kaminka, Armand, 'Beiträge zur Erklärung der Esra-Apokalypse und zur Rekonstruktion ihres hebräischen Urtextes', *Monatsschrift für Geschichte und Wissenschaft des Judentums* 76 (1932), pp. 121-38, 206-12, 494-511, 604-607; 77 (1933), pp. 339-55.
Kant, Immanuel, *Critique of Practical Reason*, trans. L.W. Beck; Indianapolis: Bobbs-Merril, The Liberal Arts Press, 1956.
Kautzsch, E., ed. *Die Apokryphen und Pseudepigraphen des Alten Testaments*, 2 vols.; 1900; rpt. Hildesheim: Georg Olms, 1962.
Keulers, Joseph, *Die eschatologische Lehre des vierten Esrabuches*, Berlin: Herder, 1922.
Klausner, Joseph, *The Messianic Idea in Israel: From Its Beginning to the Completion of the Mishnah*, trans. W.F. Stinespring; New York: Macmillan, 1955.
Klijn, A. Frederik J., ed., *Der lateinische Text der Apokalypse des Esra*, Texte und Untersuchungen zur Geschichte der altchristlichen Literature, 131; Berlin: Akademie, 1983.
—'The Sources and the Redaction of the Syriac Apocalypse of Baruch', *JSJ* 1 (1970), pp. 65-76.
—'2 (Syriac Apocalypse of) Baruch: A New Translation and Introduction', *OTP*.
—'Die syrische Baruch-Apokalypse', *Jüdische Schriften aus hellenistisch-römishcer Zeit*, 5/2; Gütersloh: Gerd Mohn, 1976.
Kmosko, M., *Epistola Baruch filli Neriae*. Patrologia Syriaca, I/2; Paris: Firmin-Didot. 1907.
Knibb, Michael A., 'Apocalyptic and Wisdom in 4 Ezra', *JSJ* 13 (1982), pp. 56-74.
—'Commentary on 2 Esdras', *The First and Second Books of Esdras*, Cambridge Bible Commentary; Cambridge: Cambridge University Press, 1979.
—'Prophecy and the Emergence of the Jewish Apocalypses', *Israel's Prophetic Heritage: Essays in Honor of Peter R. Ackroyd*, New York: Cambridge University Press, 1982.
Koch, Klaus, 'Gibt es ein Vergeltungsdogma im Alten Testament?', *ZTK* 52 (1955), pp. 1-42. English translation: 'Is There a Doctrine of Retribution in the Old Testament?', in *Theodicy in the Old Testament*. Issues in Religion and Theology, 4; ed. James L. Crenshaw; Philadelphia: Fortress, 1983.
—*The Rediscovery of Apocalyptic*, trans. Margaret Kohl; Studies in Biblical Theology, Second Series, 22; Naperville, Ill.: Allenson, 1970.
Kohler, K., 'The Essenes and the Apocalyptic Literature', *JQR* 11 (1920), pp. 145-68.
Konigsveld, P Sj. Van, 'An Arabic Manuscript of the Apocalypse of Baruch', *JSJ* 6 (1975), pp. 205-207.

Kramer, Samuel Noah, 'Man and His God': A Sumerian Variation on the "Job" Motif', *Wisdom in Israel and in the Ancient Near East*, Supplements to Vetus Testamentum, 3; Leiden: Brill, 1955.
Kuntz, J. Kenneth, 'The Retribuion Motif in Psalmic Wisdom', *ZAW* 89 (1977), pp. 223-33.
Kushner, Harold S., *When Bad Things Happen to Good People*, New York: Schocken Books, 1981.
Lambert, W.G., *Babylonian Wisdom Literature*, Oxford: Clarendon, 1960.
Mack, Burton L., 'Wisdom Myth and Mytho-logy: An Essay in Understanding a Theological Tradition', *Int* 24 (1970), pp. 46-60.
McCown, C.C., 'Hebrew and Egyptian Apocalyptic Literature', *HTR* 18 (1925), pp. 357-411.
McKane, William, *Proverbs: A New Approach*, The Old Testament Library; Philadelphia: Westminster, 1970.
McNamara, Martin, *Intertestamental Literature*, Old Testament Message, 23; Wilmington: Michael Glazier, 1983.
Metzger, Bruce M., 'The Fourth Book of Ezra: A New Translation and Introduction', *OTP*.
—*An Introduction to the Apocrypha*, New York: Oxford University Press, 1957.
—'The "Lost" Section of II Esdras (= IV Ezra)', *JBL* 76 (1957), pp. 153-56.
Millar, William R., *Isaiah 24–27 and the Origin of Apocalyptic*, Harvard Semitic Monograph Series, 11; Missoula, Mont.: Scholars Press, 1976.
Montefiore, Claude Goldsmid, *IV Ezra: A Study in the Development of Universalism*, London: George Allen & Unwin, 1929.
Moore, George Foot, *Judaism in the First Centuries of the Christian Era, the Age of the Tannaim*, 3 vols.; Cambridge, Mass.: Harvard University Press, 1950.
Morris, Leon, *Apocalyptic*, Grand Rapids: Eerdmans, 1972.
Mowinckel, Sigmund, *He That Commeth*, trans. G.W. Anderson; Nashville: Abingdon, 1954.
Müller, Hans-Peter, 'Mantische Weisheit und Apokalyptik', *Supplements to Vetus Testamentum*, 22; Leiden: Brill, 1972.
—*Ursprünge und Strukturen alttestamentlicher Eschatologie*, Berlin: Töpelmann, 1969.
Mundle, W., 'Das religiöse Problem des IV Esrabuches', *ZAW* 47 (1929), pp. 222-49.
Murdock, William R., 'History and Revelation in Jewish Apocalypticism', *Int* 21 (1967), pp. 167-87.
Myers, Jacob M., *I and II Esdras: Introduction, Translation and Commentary*, Anchor Bible, 42; Garden City, N.Y.: Doubleday, 1974.
Neusner, Jacob, 'Judaism in a Time of Crisis: Four Responses to the Destruction of the Second Temple', *Judaism* 21 (1972), pp. 313-27.
Nicholson, E.W., 'Apocalyptic', *Tradition and Interpretation: Essays by Members of the Society for Old Testamemt Study*, ed. G.W. Anderson, Oxford: Clarendon, 1979.
Nickelsburg, George W.E., 'The Apocalyptic Message of I Enoch 92–105', *CBQ* 39 (1977), pp. 309-28.
—*Jewish Literature between the Bible and the Mishnah*, Philadelphia: Fortress, 1981.
—*Resurrection, Immortality, and Eternal Life in Inter-testamental Judaism*, Harvard

Theological Studies, 26; Cambridge, Mass.: Harvard University Press, 1972.
North, Robert, 'Prophecy to Apocalyptic via Zechariah', *Supplements to Vetus Testamentum*, 22; Leiden: Brill, 1972.
Noth, Martin, 'The Understanding of History in Old Testament Apocalyptic', *The Laws in the Pentateuch and Other Studies*, trans. D.R. Ap-Thomas; Edinburgh and London: Oliver & Boyd, 1966.
Oesterley, W.O.E., *II Esdras (the Ezra Apocalypse): With Introduction and Notes*, Westminster Commentaries; London: Methuen, 1933.
von der Osten-Sacken, Peter, *Die Apokalyptik in ihrem Verhältnis zu Prophetie und Weisheit*, München: Kaiser, 1969.
Peake, Arthur S., 'Job: The Problem of the Book', *Job*, Century Bible; New York: Henry Frowde, 1905.
—*The Problem of Suffering in the Old Testament*, London: Epworth, 1904.
—'The Roots of Hebrew Prophecy and Jewish Apocalyptic', *BJRL* 7 (1923), pp. 233-55.
Petit, François, *The Problem of Evil*, trans. Christopher Williams; New York: Hawthorn, 1959.
Pfeiffer, Robert H., *History of New Testament Times: With an Introduction to the Apocrypha*, New York: Harper, 1949.
Pike, Nelson, ed., *God and Evil*, Englewood Cliffs, N.J.: Prentice-Hall, 1965.
Plöger, Otto, *Theocracy and Eschatology*, trans. S. Rudman; Oxford: Basil Blackwell, 1968.
Pritchard, James B., ed., *Ancient Near Eastern Texts Relating to the Old Testament*, 2nd edn; Princeton: Princeton University Press, 1955.
von Rad, Gerhard, 'The Confessions of Jeremiah', in *Theodicy in the Old Testament*, ed. James L. Crenshaw; Issues in Religion and Theology, 4; Philadelphia: Fortress, 1983.
—*Das Geschichtsbild des chronistischen Werkes*, Beiträge zur Wissenschaft vom alten und Neuen Testament, 54; Stuttgart: Kohlhammer, 1930.
—*The Message of the Prophets*, trans. D.M.G. Stalker; New York: Harper & Row, 1962.
—*Old Testament Theology*, II, trans. D.M.G. Stalker; New York: Harper & Row, 1965.
—*Theologie des Alten Testaments*, II, 4th edn; Munich: Kaiser, 1965.
—*Wisdom in Israel*, trans J.D. Martin; New York: Abingdon, 1972.
Rankin, O.S., *Israel's Wisdom Literature. Its Bearing on Theology and the History of Religion*, Kerr Lectures, 1933-1936; Edinburgh: T. & T. Clark, 1936.
Reicke, Bo, 'Official and Pietistic Elements of Jewish Apocalypticism', *JBL* 79 (1960), pp. 137-50.
Riessler, Paul, *Altjüdisches Schrifttum ausserhalb der Bibel*, Heidelberg: Kerle, 1928.
Rissi, Mathias, *Time and History. A Study on the Revelation*, trans. Gordon C. Winsor; Richmond, Virginia: John Knox, 1966.
Rosenthal, F., *Vier apokryphische Bücher aus der Zeit und Schule R. Akiba's*, Leipzig: Otto Schulze, 1885.
Rössler, Dietrich, *Gestz und Geschichte: Untersuchungen zur Theologie der jüdischen Apokalyptik und der pharisäischen Orthodoxie*, WMANT, 3; Düsseldorf: Neukirchener Verlag, 1960.
Rost, Leonhard, *Judaism Outside the Hebrew Canon: An Introduction to the Documents*, trans. David E. Green; Nashville: Abingdon, 1976.

Rowland, Christopher, *The Open Heaven: A Study of Apocalyptic in Judaism and Early Christianity*, New York: Crossroad, 1982.

Rowley, H.H., *The Book of Job*, The New Century Bible Commentary; Grand Rapids: Eerdmans, 1976.

—*The Relevance of Apocalyptic: A Study of Jewish and Christian Apocalypses from Daniel to the Revelation*, Greenwood, S.C.: Attic, 1963.

Russell, D.S., *The Method and Message of Jewish Apocalyptic*, The Old Testament Library; Philadelphia: Westminster, 1964.

Sanders, E.P., *Paul and Palestinian Judaism: A Comparison of Patterns of Religion*, Philadelphia: Fortress, 1977.

Sanders, Jim Alvin, *Suffering as Divine Discipline in the Old Testament and Post-Biblical Judaism*, Colgate Rochester Divinity School Bulletin, 28; Rochester, N.Y.: Colgate Rochester Divinity School, 1955.

Sayler, Gwendolyn B., *Have the Promises Failed? A Literary Analysis of 2 Baruch*, Society of Biblical Literature Dissertation Series 72; Chico, Cal: Scholars Press, 1984.

Schmid, Hans Heinrich, *Wesen und Geschiche der Weisheit: Eine Untersuchung zur altorientalischen und israelitischen Weisheitsliterature*, Berlin: Töpelmann, 1966.

Schmidt, Johann Michael, *Die jüdische Apokalyptik: Die Geschichte ihrer Erforschung von der Anfängen bis zu den Textfunden von Qumran*, 2nd edn; Düsseldorf: Neukirchener Verlag, 1976.

Schmithals, Walter, *The Apocalyptic Movement: Introduction & Interpretation*, trans. John E. Steely; Nashville: Abingdon, 1975.

Schreiner, Josef, *Alttestamentlich-jüdische Apokalyptik: Eine Einführung*, Biblische Handbibliothek, 6, München: Kösel, 1969.

Smith, Jonathan Z., 'Wisdom and Apocalyptic', *Religious Syncretism in Antiquity: Essays in Conversation with Geo Widengren*, ed. Birger A. Pearson; American Academy of Religion and The Institute of Religious Studies, University of California, Santa Barbara, Series on Formative Contemporary Thinkers, 1; Missoula, Mont.: Scholars Press, 1975.

Stamm, Johann Jakob, *Das Leiden des Unschuldigen in Babylon und Israel*, Abhandlungen zur Theologie des Alten und Neuen Testaments, 10; Zürich: Zwingli, 1946.

Stemberger, Günter, *Der Leib der Auferstehung: Studien zur Anthropologie und Eschatologie des palästinischen Judentums im neutestamentlichen Zeitalter* (*ca. 170 v. Chr.—100 n. Chr.*), Analecta Biblica, 56; Rome: Biblical Institute Press, 1972.

Stone, Michael Edward, *The Armenian Version of IV Ezra*, University of Pennsylvania Armenian Texts and Studies, 1; Missoula, Mont.: Scholars Press, 1979.

—'The Concept of the Messiah in IV Ezra', *Religions in Antiquity: Essays in Memory of Erwin Ramsdell Goodenough*, ed. Jacob Neusner; Supplements to Numen, 14; Leiden: Brill, 1968.

—'Lists of Revealed Things in the Apocalyptic Literature'. *Magnalia Dei: The Mighty Acts of God. Essays on the Bible and Archaeology in Memory of G. Ernest Wright*, ed. Frank Moore Cross, Werner E. Lemke, and Patrick D. Miller, Jr; Garden City, N.Y.: Doubleday, 1976.

—'A New Manuscript of the Syrio-Arabic Version of the Fourth Book of Ezra', *JSJ* 8 (1977), pp. 183-96.

—'Manuscripts and Readings of Armenian IV Ezra', *Textus* 6 (1968), pp. 48-61.

—'Paradise in 4 Ezra iv:8, vii:36 and viii:52', *JJS* 17 (1966), pp. 85-88.

—'Reactions to Destructions of the Second Temple: Theology, Perception and Conversion', *JSJ* 12 (1981), pp. 195-204.
—*Scriptures, Sects, and Visions: A Profile of Judaism from Ezra to the Jewish Revolts*, Philadelphia: Fortress, 1980.
—'Some Remarks on the Textual Criticism of IV Ezra', *HTR* 60 (1967), pp. 107-15.
Tennant, F.R., *The Sources of the Doctrines of the Fall and Original Sin*, Cambridge: Cambridge University Press, 1903.
Thomas, D. Winton, ed., *Documents from Old Testament Times*, London: Thomas Nelson, 1958.
Thompson, Alden L., *Responsibility for Evil in the Theodicy of IV Ezra: A Study Illustrating the Significance of Form and Structure for the Meaning of the Book*, Society of Biblical Literature Dissertation Series, 29; Missoula, Mont.: Scholars Press, 1977.
Torrey, Charles Cutler, *The Apocryphal Literature: A Brief Introduction*, New Haven: Yale University Press, 1945.
—'The Messiah Son of Ephraim', *JBL* 66 (1947), pp. 253-77.
Towner, W. Sibley, 'Retribution', *IDB, Supplementary Volume*.
—'Retributional Theology in the Apocalyptic Setting', *USQR* 26 (1971), pp. 203-14.
Turner, Nigel, 'Esdras, Books of', *IDB*, II, pp. 140-42.
Vaganay, Leon, *Le Problème eschatologique dans le IV Livre d'Esdras*, Paris: Alphonse Picard, 1906.
Vawter, Bruce, 'Apocalyptic: Its Relation to Prophecy', *CBQ* 22 (1960), pp. 33-46.
de Viliers, P.G.R., 'The Messiah and Messiahs in Jewish Apocalyptic', *Essays on Jewish and Christian Apocalyptic*, Neotestamentica 12; The New Testament Society of South Africa, 1981.
Violet, Bruno, *Die Apokalypsen des Esra und des Baruch in deutscher Gestalt*, Leipzig: Hinrichs, 1924.
—*Die Ezra-Apokalypse (IV Ezra), I. Teil: Die Überlieferung*. Die griechischen christlichen Schriftsteller der ersten drei Jahrhunderten, 18; Leipzig: Hinrichs, 1910.
Volkmar, Gustav, *Handbuch der Einleitung in die Apokryphen; Zweite Abteilung, Das vierte Buch Esra*. Tübingen: Fues, 1863.
Volz, Paul, Die Eschatologie der jüdischen Gemeinde im neutestamentlichen Zeitalter, Tübingen: J.C.B. Mohr, 1934.
Wellhausen, Julius, *Einleitung in die drei ersten Evangelien*, Berlin: Reimer, 1911.
—*Skizzen und Vorarbeiten*, 6; Berlin: Reimer, 1899.
Wicks, Henry J., *The Doctrine of God in the Jewish Apocryphal and Apocalyptic Literature*, London: Hunter & Longhurst, 1915.
Wilder, Amos N., *Eschatology and Ethics in the Teaching of Jesus*, New York: Harper, 1950.
Williams, Ronald J., 'Theodicy in the Ancient Near East', *Canadian Journal of Theology* 2 (1956), pp. 14-26.
Wolff, Hans Walter, *Joel and Amos: A Commentary on the Books of the Prophets Joel and Amos*, Hermeneia; trans. Waldemar Jansen, S. Dean McBride, Jr, and Charles A. Muenchow, ed. S. Dean McBride, Jr; Philadelphia: Fortress, 1977.
Würthwein, E., 'The Old Testament Belief in Recompense', *Theological Dictionary of the New Testament*, IV; ed. Gerhard Kittel; trans. and ed. Geoffrey W. Bromiley; Grand Rapids: Eerdmans, 1967.
Zimmermann, Frank, 'Textual Observations on the Apocalypse of Baruch', *JTS* 40 (1939), pp. 151-56.
—'Underlying Documents of IV Ezra', *JQR* 51 (1960/61), pp. 107-34.

INDEXES

INDEX OF BIBLICAL & OTHER REFERENCES

OLD TESTAMENT

NEW TESTAMENT

APOCRYPHA

OLD TESTAMENT PSEUDEPIGRAPHA

INDEX OF AUTHORS